VISITING
SMALL-TOWN
FLORIDA

Revised Edition

VISITING SMALL-TOWN FLORIDA

Revised Edition

Bruce Hunt

Pineapple Press, Inc.
Sarasota, Florida

This edition, like the original, is dedicated to my mom,
Gerry Hunt, always my biggest fan.

Inquiries should be addressed to:

Pineapple Press, Inc.
P.O. Box 3889
Sarasota, Florida 34230

www.pineapplepress.com

Library of Congress Cataloging-in-Publication Data

Hunt, Bruce.
    Visiting small-town Florida / Bruce Hunt.— Rev. ed., 1st ed.
        p.   cm.
Includes index.
    ISBN 1-56164-278-9 (alk. paper)
    1. Florida—Guidebooks. 2. Cities and towns—Florida—Guidebooks. 3. Florida—History, Local. I. Title.
    F309.3 .H86 2003
    917.5904'64—dc21

                                                                2003006309

First Edition
10 9 8 7 6 5 4 3 2 1

Design by Carol Tornatore

Printed in the United States of America

CONTENTS

Color plates are found between pages 82 and 83.

ACKNOWLEDGMENTS

I AM FORTUNATE TO BE SURROUNDED BY such good friends and family, many of whom have helped advance my writing career and all of whom have been so encouraging. I owe special thanks to Irene Maher, who got me my first television exposure; to Richard Davidson, who made introductions for me that have resulted in countless successful book signings; to my aunt Bonnie Corral, who tells everybody she knows (and that's a lot of people) about my books; to Michael Poole, who thought enough of my books to give them to every one of his clients for Christmas; to Loretta Jordan, who visited almost every one of these towns with me; and to all the folks at Pineapple Press, who do such a marvelous job of turning my thoughts and photographs into books.

FOREWORD

W HEN BRUCE HUNT ASKED if I would consider writing the foreword for his latest book, *Visiting Small-Town Florida*, I thought about his reasons for asking me. I've been a Hunt family friend for a long time, but that wasn't why he came to me. He had two other reasons. One is that I chose chamber of commerce management as my career. The other is that Bruce knows how much I love the small-town atmosphere. Although I have lived in large cities like Syracuse, New York; Cincinnati, Ohio; and Washington, DC, most of my adult life, I still yearn for the serenity and simple ways of small-town living.

I grew up in the small New England village of Anthony, Rhode Island, (population 300) on the Pawtuxet River. We had the Coventry Textile Mill (which manufactured lace), one barbershop (with one barber), one general store, a grange hall (for social functions), and one diner—the Anthony Diner, which served breakfast, lunch, and dinner. Of course, the diner was the town's daily gathering place.

Since most of Anthony's residents were Polish immigrants, the Anthony Diner served wonderful Polish meals—dumplings, borscht, shish kebab, kielbasa; their ten-cent hot-dogs were the very best I've ever had. The diner's owner would buy homemade sausages from different local town ladies, and you could request someone's sausage, specifically by name. My family's favorite was Mrs. Dlugosz's Polish sausage, and we asked for it whenever we ate there. Everyone knew everyone else in town, and the diner was the place to catch up on the latest goings-on.

Such is the climate in small towns. It's charming. It's close-knit. Sometimes it's nosy, but when one family needs help, the whole community pitches in.

I have been back to Anthony, Rhode Island, to visit, a number of times. It has, like most of Rhode Island, been absorbed by that state's largest city, Providence—no surprise, since all of Rhode Island is no bigger than Hillsborough County, Florida. As a result, it has lost some of its once-wonderful, small-town atmosphere.

In 1957, I brought my family to Tampa and began working for the Greater Tampa Chamber of Commerce. I was president during my last twenty-one years, until I retired in 1993. Chambers of commerce help guide and manage the economic, social, and cultural growth of cities, large and small. I also worked closely with the United States Chamber of Commerce. With them, my charge was to help small community organizations plan for the future. This gave me the opportunity to meet and talk with lots of community leaders in small towns. Many of them reminded me of the people I grew up with in Anthony.

At the Tampa Chamber of Commerce I had fifty people on staff. Small-town chambers are often a one-person show. In my opinion, the small-town chamber's task is a more difficult one.

I still live in Tampa, and it's a wonderful, growing, thriving city and an interesting place to live. It has all the amenities that larger cities offer, but a part of me still desires the charm and uniqueness of a small town, where I know everybody by name, and they all know me—a place where I can drop in at the busy little diner down on Main Street (maybe the only diner in town) every morning and have breakfast with the locals.

Visiting Small-Town Florida is a terrific source of information and anecdotes about Florida's most quaint, picturesque, and historic small towns. Reading it has made me nostalgic. Some of the towns and villages I have visited before, but others I have never been to, even though I've lived in Florida for thirty-eight years. I plan to take some long, get-away-for-the-weekend trips, as Bruce suggests, to those that I haven't seen. Maybe I'll find that perfect small town, the one that I've been quietly thinking about for so many years. You might enjoy doing the same.

Al Trayner
Greater Tampa Chamber of Commerce, Retired
1957–1993, President 1972–1993

Author's note: Al Trayner wrote this Foreword for Volume 1 of *Visiting Small-Town Florida*. He did such a great job of capturing the essence of small-towndom that I decided to repeat it for this edition.

INTRODUCTION

I HAD NO IDEA, WHEN I FIRST CONSIDERED writing *Visiting Small-Town Florida*, that there would be so many others who felt the same draw to these out-of-the-way places that I did. That original volume, which came out in 1997, quickly went into multiple printings, and Pineapple Press asked if I would write *Visiting Small-Town Florida* Volume 2 (1999) to include towns not in the first volume. As I did book signings, talks, and slide shows to promote the books, I met scores of people who had fallen in love with the quaintness, peacefulness, and eccentricity of Florida's small towns. From those, like me, who live in large, urban areas, I heard a recurring sentiment: whatever advantages the big city once offered were now being outweighed by its complications—crime, crowding, traffic jams, long lines, and rampant rudeness. People were longing for a simpler lifestyle, one still commonplace in those hamlets and boroughs that are fortunate enough to be inconvenient to Florida's main thoroughfares. Small towns offered neighborliness, safety, a sense of belonging to a community, a sense of living in a place that has its own identity, and, just as important, a little elbow room. Not everyone could pull up stakes and move to one of these great small towns, but they *could* visit.

Like previous volumes of *Visiting Small-Town Florida*, this revised edition is a guide for visitors to Florida's tucked-away towns and quaint communities, places with names like Sopchoppy, Ozello, Yeehaw Junction, and Two Egg. I must confess that I have sometimes taken liberty with the term "town." Some of these places are mere crossroads, but I have included them because they are the kinds of places that make the journey as intriguing as the destination. While you may not spend a full vacation or even a full weekend there, these dots on the map are nonetheless well worth plotting your route through. Other places—the ones with bed-and-breakfasts, restaurants, antiques shops, and museums—do qualify as destinations and merit longer visits. Like most guidebooks, this one provides all the pertinent information: directions, addresses, phone numbers, web sites, things to see and do, and places to stay and dine. Unlike most guidebooks, it also contains some of my own experiences when I visited these places. I met some interesting folks along the way and I've recounted snippets of our conversations. And, because each town's personality is so intertwined with its past, I dug into their histories and pulled out the most interesting tidbits. Call it a travelogue, if you will.

How did I define "small town" for the purposes of this book? I looked for towns that haven't been swallowed up by the spreading megalopolises and that have a population of fewer than ten thousand people (based on the 2000 census). Most of the towns have fewer than two thousand people. My population cutoff caused some consternation for me this time. Two of my favorites, Fernandina Beach and Lake Wales, fell off the list because their population now exceeds ten thousand. Bok Tower Gardens in Lake Wales is one of the most beautiful and serene places in Florida. Fernandina Beach on Amelia Island—with its rich history, great B & Bs, and outstanding restaurants—is still one of my favorite weekend destinations. Although I considered bumping up my cutoff point so I could include Fernandina Beach and Lake Wales, ultimately I decided to hold true to my original parameters.

This revised edition combines the towns of both previous volumes, minus one or two as mentioned. There are also a couple of additions. Many of the towns that I visited or revisited in these pages have one or more festivals during the year (these are listed in the Appendix). However, I tried to time my research visits when there was no special event because I wanted to give you a sense of what each town is like on any normal day.

Admittedly, not all of Florida's small towns are interesting to visit, but the ones included here are. Each has its own personality. Most, like Micanopy, have been around for a long time; others, like Seaside, are relatively new. I have written in great detail about some; for others, I've picked just one or two highlights to feature—more often than not, a good place to eat. More than one critic has accused me of writing *Eating*

Your Way Across Small-Town Florida. It's true. I'm always on the hunt for a great little hole-in-the-wall diner or local-cuisine restaurant. My eatery picks rarely require a reservation (and never a jacket).

So turn the page and follow winding back roads to seventy of Florida's most fascinating and often eccentric small towns. Each chapter is a minor journey, an exploration, an escape. Along the way, you'll see some interesting sights, meet some unusual and endearing characters, and learn a little about each place's past. I'll take you to museums and galleries, down scenic paths, and through historic neighborhoods, where you can marvel at the intricate architecture of past centuries. I'll tell you about some wonderful places to stay and, of course, great places to eat. I'll also point out unique shops where you can find antiques, old books, curios, and arts and crafts. Between the lines there are other stories being told—not by me but by the sometimes-humorous, often-opinion-ated, but always gracious and welcoming people who have chosen to spend their lives in these towns. Theirs are stories about pursuing happiness, about deciding to improve the quality of their lives, and often about following a less conventional path toward achieving those things.

NORTH REGION

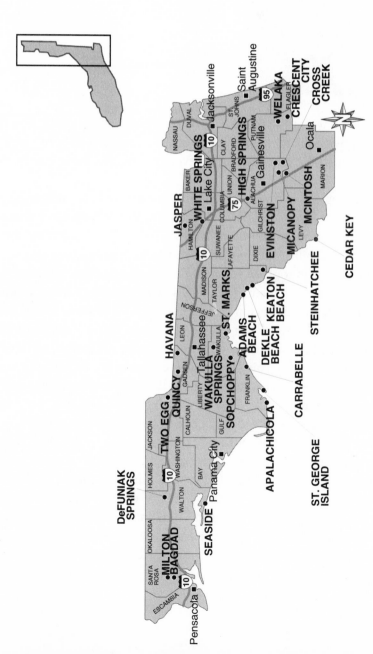

MILTON AND BAGDAD

Population: Milton 7,045   Bagdad 1,490

MILTON AND BAGDAD—THE TWO TOWNS THAT PINE TREES BUILT. You can't discuss one without mentioning the other. Separated only by the Pond Creek bayou, their histories and development are inextricably intertwined.

This was logging and sawmill country as early as 1817, when the King of Spain granted land along Pond Creek to Juan de la Rua. De la Rua built and operated a lumber mill there for ten years before becoming discouraged with his inability to keep laborers. In 1828, he sold his property to Joseph Forsyth, who took on partners Ezekiel and Andrew Simpson. They built the dam-driven Arcadia Mill, and a village began to grow around it. The vast forests of this region were thick with valuable long-leaf yellow pine, and the Blackwater River provided a ready highway for floating logs down to Pensacola Bay. Forsyth and the Simpsons prospered, and in 1840 they moved the mill a couple of miles downstream to the juncture of Pond Creek and the Blackwater River. A village grew around it again. This time it took on the name Bagdad—perhaps because, like its Middle Eastern namesake, it was wedged between two important rivers.

Bagdad grew up on the south side of Pond Creek, and Milton grew up on the north side. About the same time that Joseph Forsyth and the Simpson brothers were getting the Arcadia Mill into full swing, Benjamin and Margaret Jernigan were starting a mill of their own. People began to refer to the area around it as Jernigan's Landing and also as Scratch Ankle, presumably because of the dense briars that grew along the banks of the Blackwater River. Neither of those names stuck, but a more definitive one,

2

Milltown, did, and it eventually evolved into Milton, which was incorporated in 1844.

More sawmills opened over the next few decades. By the turn of the century, Milton and Bagdad had become the most industrialized towns in Florida. The lumber barons thought the bounty was endless, but they were short-sighted. The Crash of 1929 hit both towns hard. Plus, the once-plentiful pine forests had become depleted. The last of the mills, the Bagdad Land & Lumber Company, closed in 1939.

Santa Rosa County Road 191 becomes Forsyth Street for a brief dozen or so blocks as it rolls into Bagdad from the south. On the right, behind a hedge, is the stately, pre–Civil War Thompson House. Mill owner Benjamin Thompson built the two-story antebellum mansion, with its double front porches and twelve white columns. During the Civil War, invading Union troops commandeered the house. By then most of the townspeople had fled. Before moving on, they left a message, scrawled in charcoal across a wall in the parlor, that is still there today: "Mr. Thompson, Spurling's First Cavalry camped in your house on the 26th of October, 1864." Originally the house overlooked the Blackwater River, a few blocks to the east, but in 1912 the owners must have wanted a change of scenery. They jacked the house up onto log rollers, turned it around 180 degrees, and pulled it by mule to its present location. The D'Asaro family, the house's current owners, built removable paneling in the parlor to preserve the historic scribblings.

Across the road and around the corner on Thompson Street is the old Bagdad Post Office, a tiny wooden building with only one window. It belongs to the Bagdad Village Preservation Association. Right now it is being prepped for restoration. The building went into service in 1913 and closed in 1986. Four blocks south and a block west of Forsyth Street, at the corner of Bushnell and Church Streets, is the Bagdad Village Preservation Association's museum in a building that was once Bagdad's first African-American church (see photo on page 2).

Across Pond Creek Bridge, Milton has grown into a sizable town, with a population of more than seven thousand. The downtown district has been nicely renovated, particularly Caroline Street (Highway 90) and Willing Street, which parallels the Blackwater River. Downtown reminds me of a miniature Savannah or New Orleans French Quarter. Riverwalk

Park—with its pink-blossoming crepe myrtle trees, brick walkways, wrought-iron-and-wood park benches, gas lamp–style street lights, and a dock—lines the waterfront behind Willing Street.

Devastating fires swept through the downtown in 1909 and again in 1911, leveling much of the district. But this was boom time in Milton, and the town was rebuilt bigger and better than before. Two notable brick buildings—the three-story Imogene Theater on Caroline Street between Elmira and Willing Streets and the Exchange Hotel at the corner of Caroline and Elmira Streets—were part of Milton's rebirth from the ashes.

Architect Walker Willis designed the theater. It was originally called the Milton Opera House when it opened in 1912. When the Gootch family bought it in 1920, they renamed it after their eleven-year-old daughter, Imogene. A post office and a store shared the first floor. The upstairs theater ran vaudeville shows and silent movies and later "talkies" until it closed in 1946. The Santa Rosa Historical Society restored it in 1987. Its offices, along with the Milton Opera House

*The 1913/1914 Exchange Hotel in Milton is now
the First Judicial State Attorney's office.*

Museum of Local History, now occupy a portion of the building.

Charles Sudmall, who operated the local telephone exchange, was so impressed with the Milton Opera House that he hired the same contractor, S. F. Fulguhm Company of Pensacola, to build the Exchange Hotel in 1913. Sudmall insisted that the hotel architecturally match the Opera House. The hotel closed around 1946, but it was restored in 1984 and is now the First Judicial Circuit State Attorney's Office.

From downtown, I follow Caroline Street (Highway 90) west, past Pensacola Junior College, then turn north onto Anna Simpson Road, and west again onto Mill Pond Road, which dead-ends at a trailhead for the Arcadia Mill Archeological Site. On the left, a driveway leads up to the Arcadia Mill Site Museum.

Warren Weekes, the museum's curator, told me about Arcadia in the 1840s. "Back then, you were not allowed to acquire property and then turn right around to resell it. When Juan de la Rua got this property from the King of Spain, he had to keep it, improve it, and work it for a minimum of seven years. He paid the King of Spain one shipload of square lumber per year in taxes. When de la Rua sold the property to John Forsyth for four hundred dollars, he was glad to get rid of it. De la Rua wasn't much for running the mill. He was more interested in politics—went on later to become mayor of Pensacola. The Arcadia Mill ran off of two big water wheels driven by Pond Creek. The mill made square lumber with straight saws—the round saw wasn't invented until after eighteen forty. They would cut the long-leaf yellow pine lengthwise, flip it on its side, then cut it again so that it came out square."

Forsyth moved the mill in 1840 when he acquired a steam engine to replace the water wheels. The engine allowed him to set up the mill at the mouth of the river, which facilitated transporting the lumber. The Arcadia Mill Site Museum displays a collection of old photographs from the mill's era, as well as artifacts excavated from the Arcadia site by the University of West Florida's Archaeology Department.

The trail leads into the woods, over a rise, and down into a ravine, where it crosses a swinging wooden bridge spanning Pond Creek. This was the site of the Arcadia Mill dam and water wheels. Beneath the clear water of Pond Creek, I can still see the remains of a rock wall—a part of what was once the foundation of the dam—built into the bank of the creek.

*The 1909 Milton Railroad Depot was restored by the Santa Rosa Historical
Society and reopened on July 4, 1976.*

Back on County Road 191, another restored Milton historical structure,
the 1909 Milton Railroad Depot, sits next to railroad tracks just across
the Pond Creek Bridge. Although trains still run on these tracks, they no
longer stop here. The original depot, built in 1882, burned in 1907. The
1909 depot was part of the Louisville and Nashville Railroad system.
When passenger trains were discontinued in 1973, the depot closed and
fell quickly into disrepair. The following year, the Santa Rosa Historical
Society was formed to save it. The depot reopened on July 4, 1976. It
now houses the West Florida Railroad Museum and a model railroad
shop.

DIRECTIONS: From I-10, take Santa Rosa CR 191 north.

DON'T MISS: Riverwalk Park in Milton
ADDRESSES AND EVENTS: See page 189

DeFUNIAK
SPRINGS

Population: 5,089

FREDERICK DEFUNIAK WAS PRESIDENT OF THE Pensacola and Atlantic sub-sidiary of the Louisville and Nashville (L & N) Railroad in the 1880s. It is fitting that DeFuniak Springs bears his name, since the railroad estab-lished the town in 1881 and actively promoted its recreational offerings.

Baldwin Avenue is the main street of DeFuniak Springs' historic dis-trict. It runs east and west just across the railroad tracks from Lake DeFuniak. Freshly restored brick storefronts face south and overlook the lake and the restored L & N train depot, now home to the Walton County Heritage Museum. Chipley Park, on the north side of Lake DeFuniak, has an open-air amphitheater and band shell. Large, gracious Victorian homes, many built before the turn of the twentieth century, line Circle Drive, which surrounds the almost perfectly round, spring-fed Lake DeFuniak, which is one mile in circumference.

In 1884, the Chautauqua Association chose DeFuniak Springs as its winter assembly location. The Chautauqua Association, based in Lake Chautauqua, New York, promoted a combination of adult education, recreation, and religion. The Florida Chautauqua Association was formed and had a substantial, long-term influence on education and society in DeFuniak Springs.

In 1886, a group of local women in DeFuniak Springs started a library to support the needs of the Florida Chautauqua Association. Renamed the Walton-DeFuniak Library in 1975, it's the oldest, contin-uously operated library in Florida. Located on the inside of Circle Drive, it sits overlooking Lake DeFuniak about a quarter of the way around.

7

Walton-DeFuniak Public Library on Circle Drive

The hardwood-frame building is simple with some pleasing exterior motifs typical of the time it was built, such as the diagonal slats on the upper portion of the outside walls and scalloped shingles in the front gable over the entranceway. The original front section of the building was completed in 1887 at a cost of $580. A rear section was added in 1984 but blends so well architecturally that it appears to be part of the original.

Inside, polished wood floors and large, oval throw rugs give the library a warm feeling. An amazing display of old swords, spears, battle axes, crossbows, and muskets hangs on the walls. The collection originally belonged to Professor Kenneth Bruce from Palmer College in DeFuniak Springs, who left the armaments to the college in his will. When Palmer College closed its doors in the 1930s, the collection was given to the city and later passed on to the library. Many of the weapons are European and date back to the Crusades (A.D. 1100–1300), while some pieces come from Malaysia, Persia, and Japan. The Kentucky muskets date from the mid to late 1700s.

More historic buildings and homes surround Lake DeFuniak. Just past the library is the 1909 Chautauqua Building, originally the Chautauqua

St. Agatha's Episcopal Church on Circle Drive

Hall of Brotherhood, that today houses the Walton County Chamber of Commerce. Circle Drive continues past St. Agatha's Episcopal Church, with its ornate, stained-glass windows. Built in 1896, it's the oldest church on the circle. In the next block, at 219 Circle Drive, you'll find the Bullard House, a three-story, turn-of-the-century Victorian complete with bay windows and a turret with a steeple (see photo on page 7).

Shops and cafés fill the restored buildings on and around Baldwin Avenue. The Book Store, with its large selection of new and used books, anchors the east end. A couple of blocks west you can't miss The Big Store in the century-old building that was originally the General Store and Mercantile. It's now filled with antiques and flowers. Just across the railroad tracks on Crescent Drive, you'll find Dee South's enormous collection of antique porcelain, crystal, jewelry, and furniture at Southebys Antiques. One room contains nothing but teacups, saucers, and teakettles. Two great places to grab lunch are Murray's Café, on the corner of Sixth and Baldwin (try the fried green tomato sandwich and homemade cakes), and the Busy Bee, a block off Baldwin on Seventh.

One hundred years ago, DeFuniak Springs was a place that successfully combined Southern, small-town charm with sophistication, culture, and education. Today's residents have done (and continue to do) an exceptional job of restoring that heritage.

DIRECTIONS: Take I-10 to the Highway 331/DeFuniak Springs exit (Exit 85). Go north 3 miles to Highway 90 (Nelson Avenue) and drive another mile west to the downtown historic district.

DON'T MISS: Walton-DeFuniak Library
ADDRESSES AND EVENTS: see page 189

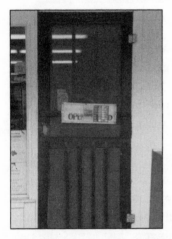

TWO EGG

Population: 31

ONE HALF BLOCK FROM THE JUNCTION OF Jackson County Road 69 and County Road 69A (better known locally as Wintergreen Road), the Lawrence Grocery Store sits at the center of all activity in Two Egg, Florida. Actually, it's the only activity in Two Egg. At one time, the Pittman Store across the street competed with it, but that's been closed since Mr. Pittman retired in 1984.

Nell Lawrence King has owned the Lawrence Grocery since 1988. It has been in her family for the better part of four decades. Her father, her uncle, and her brothers have all owned it at one time or another. The first time I walked through the screen door, Nell smiled and welcomed me with a "Howdy." I didn't want her to think I was with the IRS or anything, so I explained that I was gathering research for my book on small towns.

"I've lived within a couple miles of here all my life," Nell told me. "This is the entire town of Two Egg. Let me count up for a second and I'll tell you what the population is." For about five seconds, Nell mentally ticked off in her head who had had babies lately. "Should be twenty-eight right now. Yeah, we may be a small town, but people do know we're here. The Florida Department of Transportation folks over in Tallahassee tell us that the 'Two Egg' road sign out on CR sixty-nine is the most stolen road sign in the whole state."

"You already know what my first question is going to be, don't you?" I asked Nell.

"Yep," she responded. "How did it get to be named Two Egg? It is Two Egg, by the way, not Two Eggs. It was originally named Allison. Back in the eighteen nineties, a salesman who stopped here frequently on his

Nell Lawrence King's Lawrence Grocery Store in Two Egg

route started calling it Two Egg. Every time he would come into the store, he would see the little children of a local farm-working family, the Williamses, bringing in eggs to trade for sodas or candy. It was a large family. Each child had a chicken to care for and, in lieu of an allowance, they could use the eggs from their chickens to barter at the store. The smaller children could just manage one egg in each hand, hence the name Two Egg. Mr. Will Williams comes in here to sit and visit regularly. He says it was his grandfather's children—Will's aunts and uncles—who traded eggs at the store back then. Will tells me that his grandfather had fifty-seven children by three wives."

Customers came and went while we talked. Nell knew each of them on a first-name basis. I noticed that with some customers there was no exchange of money, and I asked Nell why.

"Well, it's something you don't see hardly anymore, but we still run an account for our regular customers. In addition to groceries, we sell gas, oil, batteries, hardware, nuts and bolts. This is peanut farming territory, so we get a lot of business from the farmers. My local customers come from within about a ten-mile radius of here. Oftentimes they'll sit for a while and have coffee and talk. Plus, I get tourists in here every day. In the summer, the tour buses stop here. I sell a lot of Two Egg caps and T-shirts."

When I asked Nell if she'd ever had anyone famous stop in, she pulled a thick guest book out from under the counter and went directly to a page from September 1992. She pointed to Faye Dunaway's signature. "You know, she was raised in Bascom, about six miles north of here," Nell explained. "She went to school with my husband. When she came in to the store in ninety-two, she stayed for a good thirty minutes and talked to all the customers who came in. She was interested to know if any of them had known her dad."

Nell's father walked in and pulled up a chair. I asked him about the history of the store, and he said that Mathis Pittman built the store and owned it for quite some time before selling it to the Powell family. Mr. Lawrence bought it from Johnny Powell in the mid-1960s.

On my most recent visit to Two Egg, I found that not much had changed (and that's a good thing). Nell re-counted the population for me. "Up to thirty-one now," she told me. "Oh, and we have a second 'Two Egg' sign a block down the road facing north on sixty-nine A now."

The store looked just as I remembered it, with the addition of a couple of new items on the shelf: local cane syrup from Robert E. Long Cane Syrup, just around the corner on Highway 69, and a selection of Two Egg oil paintings by Bascom artist Marion Oswald.

Nell continues her family's tradition and points out that she has now owned the store longer than any of the other Lawrences. Six days a week she opens at 6:30 in the morning and closes at 7:00 in the evening, sometimes later if folks are chatting.

DIRECTIONS: From I-10 east of Marianna, take Jackson CR 69 north to CR 69A.

DON'T MISS: Two Egg! Don't blink or you will!
ADDRESSES AND EVENTS: see page 190

QUINCY

Population: 6,982

APPROACHING QUINCY FROM THE EAST, Highway 12 glides over rolling hills and past oak trees densely spider-webbed with kudzu. It's a reminder that the topography at this northern end of the state blends seamlessly with southern Alabama and southern Georgia. The town of Quincy does the same thing.

Quincy's entire downtown and most of the surrounding residential area have been designated a National Register Historic District. Quincy is the Gadsden County seat, and like so many small towns in the heart of the South, it has a stately dome-topped courthouse with four massive white columns in the middle of the town square. The courthouse has been in continuous use since 1827. A Civil War monument on the south side of the courthouse reads, "Sacred to the memory of the Confederate soldiers from Gadsden County, Florida, who died in the defense of their country."

One of the fifty-five historic structures in the district is the 1912 Bell & Bates Hardware Store Building on North Madison Street, on the east side of the town square. The Bates family still owns the hardware business, and in 1997 they built a modern building on Duval Street behind the original. That same year, they donated the original 1912 building to Gadsden Arts, Incorporated, which restored it and opened it in 2000 as the Gadsden Art Center, a gallery and educational exhibit center.

Around the corner on East Washington Street is the 1949 Leaf Theatre Building, originally a movie theater named in honor of the shade tobacco that was grown in this area for cigar wrappers (see next chapter on Havana). The movie theater closed in 1980. Through private donations and grants, it was restored and reopened in 1983 as a performing arts theater, and the Quincy Music Theatre has hosted musical productions here ever since. The theater has fifteen rows of seats plus a balcony, and its deep-set stage includes a revolving center.

The surrounding neighborhood is filled with both pre– and post–Civil War homes. A historic walking tour pamphlet, available from the Chamber of Commerce or at the Gadsden Art Center, is the best guide to finding these gems. A few of historical and architectural note are the Queen Anne Victorian McFarlin House (see photo page 13) on East King Street, built by tobacco planter John McFarlin in 1895 and now a bed-and-breakfast; the Allison House, also a bed-and-breakfast, on North Madison Street, built in 1843 by General A. K. Allison, who would serve as governor of Florida in 1865; and the red-brick Quincy Academy Building on North Adams Street, built in 1851 and now the Presbyterian Community Service Building.

There is an interesting historical side note that connects Quincy with the Coca-Cola Company. In the early 1900s, patrons of the Quincy State Bank, Florida's first chartered state bank, were told by Mark

Restored 1851 Quincy Academy building

Munroe, the bank's president, that purchasing stock in a fledgling drink company might prove to be a good investment. Lots of Quincyites took his advice and became wealthy. For many years, residents in Quincy held more than half of Coca-Cola's outstanding shares. Today they are still thought to own as much as ten percent of Coca-Cola's stock.

DIRECTIONS: From I-10, take the Highway 267 exit (Exit 181) and go north.

DON'T MISS: The Gadsden Art Center
ADDRESSES AND EVENTS: see page 190

HAVANA

Population: 1,713

BEFORE KEITH HENDERSON AND LEE HOTCHKISS came along, Havana had been a boarded-up ghost town for nearly twenty years. That's Havana, Florida, twelve miles north of Tallahassee. Locals pronounce it "*Hay-van-a*."

In 1981, Keith and Lee, husband-and-wife antiques shop owners from Tallahassee, came looking for an affordable building where they could relocate their shop. When I interviewed them in 1998, Lee told me, "We originally were just interested in the one corner building, but the owners wanted to sell the whole block and made us such an attractive offer that we bought it all. We talked to all our antique-business friends in Tallahassee about the idea of an antique district in downtown Havana. They loved it, and four of them decided to move their stores here and rent space in the block! We spent that entire summer and fall renovating. We sandblasted six coats of this awful green paint off the walls. We pulled out the drop ceiling, pulled out all the drywall so that the brick interior walls would show. We put in the wood floors, built cabinets and shelves. It was a chore, and we did it all ourselves. The first weekend we opened up, there were five shops in the block. It was a hit from day one!"

Keith and Lee's shop, H & H Antiques, occupies the bottom floor of a restored 1908 two-story brick building on the northwest corner of their "block" at Seventh Avenue and Main Street (Highway 27). Jasmine ivy grows across the front entrance, up to the second floor, and then around the corner. An old stained-glass window adjacent to the front

16

door depicts a barmaid serving Molly Malone beer. Although Keith and Lee sell all kinds of antiques, including stained glass, they concentrate on furniture, both new and antique. Recently they became a Norwalk Furniture dealer.

Another of Keith and Lee's projects was the McLauchlin House, a large, restored dogwalk floor plan farmhouse one block west of H & H Antiques. It has a wide, covered wraparound porch with ornate, Victorian gingerbread trim and houses six different shops selling antiques, furniture, and clothing. When I asked Keith about the house, a smile formed on his face. "That's an interesting story," he told me. "The McLauchlin House was built in the eighteen forties. It was on a farm about twenty miles north of here in Decatur County, Georgia. One of the residents here in Havana, Nellie McLauchlin Cantey, was born in the house in eighteen ninety-nine. She also married her husband, Joe Cantey, in the house in nineteen nineteen. When Nellie's brother passed away, the family considered selling the farm. Lee and I went up there to buy some of the furniture, and we just fell in love with the house. We talked to them about buying it, along with some of the acreage. It turns out that the family really wanted to keep the property, but no one was

The McLauchlin House, a circa-1840s "dogwalk-style" farmhouse, was restored and relocated from Decatur County, Georgia, to Havana. It's now an antiques shop.

going to live in the house. Then Nellie came up with a wonderful plan. She offered to give us the house on two conditions: one, that we pay the expense to move the house, and two, that we move it to Havana, where she could be near it. Needless to say, we accepted her offer. The house movers had to cut it into three sections to transport it. In nineteen ninety-four, not long after we finished fixing it up, Nellie and Joe celebrated their seventy-fifth wedding anniversary in the house."

From 1981 on, Havana was a town reborn. Its downtown district and surrounding neighborhood were richly restored. Dozens of antiques shops, art galleries, and quaint cafés turned it into a destination for browsers from all over the South. Among my favorite Havana shops is Rita and Jim Love's Little River General Store (see photo page 16), just around the corner from H & H on Main Street. In keeping with the true definition of a general store, they have a little bit of everything in here: food (lots of sauces and spices), an entire counter full of candy, shelves of dry goods, soaps, cookware, kerosene lamps, gardening tools, kitchen utensils, and toys. What makes their inventory unusual is that it seems Rita and Jim have traveled through a time machine to acquire it. Black licorice, jawbreakers, and bubble gum cigars occupy the candy case. They have Necco wafers and moon pies, and nostalgic toys like Lincoln Logs, erector sets, and Radio Flyer wagons. The store's brick walls, wood-plank floors, and wood tables and display counters add to the old-fashioned atmosphere.

Next door is another unusual shop, Mirror Image Antiques. They have a tiny art gallery in a walk-in vault and a great collection of old baseball cards and old cameras, but most fascinating is their Pete Peterson collection of Oriental antiques. Pete Peterson was the United States ambassador to Viet Nam just after the war. Pieces in the collection—some dating to the fifteenth century—come from Viet Nam, China, and Bali. Beare's Books 'N Things, a block away on Seventh Avenue, has an inventory of fifteen thousand antiquarian and out-of-print books with a particular specialization in books on history, political, military, and the Civil War.

Havana's revitalization spread across Main Street (Highway 27), where more shops and restaurants have opened. The Cannery, on East Eighth Avenue, is a red-brick canning warehouse that was renovated in the mid-1990s and converted into a complex of restaurants, shops, and

*The Cannery in Havana, remodeled into a restaurant and shops complex,
once housed the Havana Canning Company, which supplied canned fruits
and vegetables to U.S. troops during World War II.*

hundreds of individual antiques booths. It's a maze—actually several
warehouse buildings connected to one another. Back in the early 1940s,
Mrs. Eulia Stephens decided to expand her home canning business into
a full-fledged fruit and vegetable packing plant. Vegetable growing was
big business around Havana in those days. With the start of World War
II and the demand for foods with a long shelf life to feed the troops, the
Havana Canning Company was canning nearly seven million pounds of
fruit and vegetables a year. When the canning business faded in the early
1960s, Cal Albritton bought the facility to pack his Tupelo honey.

The people of Havana have done a remarkable job of creating something new from the remains of its old. The town was originally incorporated in 1906 and was named in honor of the Cuban tobacco that had
been widely cultivated in this area during the previous three quarters of
a century. In later years, tobacco farmers in Havana specialized in growing "shade tobacco," the leaves of which cigar makers use as the outer
wrapper of cigars. They called it shade tobacco because they grew it
under cheesecloth tarps, which let just the right amount of light

through in order to grow perfect leaves. The harvested leaves were then carefully dried over charcoal-pit fires. The entire operation was a delicate process. In the mid-1960s, under a foreign goodwill program sponsored by the United States government, the north Florida shade tobacco growers' special farming and harvesting techniques were taught to workers in several South American countries. Within just a couple of years, these countries were producing shade tobacco at a significantly lower cost, and the growing industry around Havana (and, consequently, the town itself) died. It would be almost two more decades before Keith Henderson and Lee Hotchkiss would come along and begin CPR on Havana's downtown district.

There's a variety of excellent restaurants in Havana. One of my favorites, the Nicholson Farmhouse Restaurant, requires a three-mile drive east of town on State Road 12. Scottish immigrant Dr. Malcolm Nicholson was a prominent physician and planter who was active in the early development of the north central region of Florida. He was on the original committee that chose Tallahassee as Florida's state capital in 1824. He built his seven-room plantation farmhouse—among the oldest houses in Gadsden County—sometime around 1828, using lumber from pine trees on his own property. Hand-formed bricks were stacked inside its wood-frame walls for added insulation.

The farm remained in the Nicholson family until 1971, when it was sold to the Eubanks family, who did a lot of restoration work on the house. Paul Nicholson, great-great-grandson of Dr. Malcolm Nicholson, and Paul's wife, Ann, bought the house back in 1987, along with the surrounding fifty acres, and opened the restaurant. The farmhouse, the adjacent smokehouse, and a barn are original buildings. Paul and Ann relocated several more vintage buildings to the property: the Littman farmhouse, built in 1890, from a couple of miles down State Road 12; the Shady Rest Tourist Camp building (it looks like an old Wild West hotel), built in 1927, also from just down the road; and the Overstreet, Florida, Post Office/Patrick's General Store. Overstreet is near the coast about halfway between Apalachicola and Panama City. Thomas Patrick built the structure in 1916, and members of the Patrick family operated it continuously until 1991. Paul and Ann purchased it and moved it to the Nicholson farm in 1995.

The 1828 Nicholson Farmhouse Restaurant near Havana was once the home of north Florida pioneer Dr. Malcolm Nicholson.

The farmhouse's décor includes a mixture of wood-frame and brick walls with solid pine beams across the ceiling. It feels like a home. After all, that's what it was for more than a century. Sadly, Paul Nicholson died in an automobile accident while on a hunting trip in Argentina in 1999. Gerald and Teresa Carpenter now own the restaurant and have kept it much the same as it was under Paul Nicholson's ownership.

Steaks are the Nicholson Farmhouse specialty. They cut and age their own beef. Although I don't ordinarily assassinate a good steak with steak sauce, I did sample some of the Nicholson Farmhouse's own sauce on my tenderloin fillet. It's made with Vidalia onions, vinegar, mustard, tomatoes, and something else (unidentified) that gives it a tangy, sweet flavor. My entrée came with a baked stuffed potato, whipped with cheese and sour cream to a soufflé consistency; a salad with whole pickled okra; fresh green beans; and hot-out-of-the-oven rolls, all of which was superb, as was my peanut butter pie for dessert.

After dinner, I walked through the Nicholson-Freeman Cemetery on the east side of the property. Dr. Malcolm Nicholson shares a headstone with his wife, Mary. The epitaph on one side reads, "Called the Father of Medicine in Florida."

DIRECTIONS: Travel 12 miles north of Tallahassee on Highway 27.

DON'T MISS: The Little River General Store and the Nicholson Farmhouse Restaurant
ADDRESSES AND EVENTS: See page 191

SEASIDE

Population: 100 (estimated)

THE QUAINT BEACHSIDE COMMUNITIES OF Seagrove, Grayton Beach, and Seaside are in stark contrast to the neon tackiness of Panama City, only forty-five minutes to the east. County Road 30A rolls along at the whim of the shoreline. Both the highway and the homes alongside it sit atop the fifteen-foot bluff that drops off to the beach. From this slightly elevated position, the Gulf water glows a rich shade of emerald. Sea oats and wind-stunted scrub oaks sprout from the dunes. Just west of Seagrove is Seaside, the eighty-acre town of wood-framed, tin-roofed, screen-porched Florida beach cottages in every color the folks at Crayola ever imagined. If there's a waiting station at the Pearly Gates, this is probably what it looks like.

Robert Davis spent his childhood summers in the 1950s on the beach at Seagrove, near eighty acres of undeveloped land that his grandfather, J. S. Smolian, had purchased in 1946. A Birmingham, Alabama, department store owner, Smolian envisioned building an employee summer camp on the property and later considered building a conference center with cottages, but neither project came to fruition. In 1978, Robert Davis inherited the property from his grandfather. Davis ultimately decided to use some of his grandfather's ideas for developing the land but expanded on them greatly. The result was Seaside.

By design, Seaside is a walking town with brick streets and sand-and-shell pathways. There is no mowable grass, except in the center of the town square—only native scrub oaks, shrubs, loblolly pines, and palm trees. All of the cottages (actually, some of them qualify as mansions, by my definition) are built in a similar, Florida-beach-bungalow vernacular style, but no two are even remotely alike. There are surprises around every corner. Each time I visit, I find myself repeating, "Oooh, that's a neat idea!" White picket fences (a code requirement) of all different styles front each home, and gingerbread details on the porches and windows add character. The homes are cozy and close together, yet owners retain sufficient privacy. This is a rope-hammocks-and-rocking-chairs kind of place. Front porches (another requirement), second- and third-floor porches, and rooftop gazebos on some of the cottages have postcard views of the beach and the Gulf. Amazingly, Seaside's very restrictive building and architectural code actually seems to open the door to diversity, individuality, and imagination. With houses painted in pastel blue, turquoise, yellow, pink, and purple, I feel like I'm walking through a watercolor painting. Across County Road 30A, on the beach side, nine distinct and architecturally dramatic open-air pavilions with boardwalks invite residents across the dunes and down onto the beach.

Some of Seaside's residents are year-round, but for most this is their second home. Many of the cottages can be rented through the Seaside Cottage Rental Agency. There's also a terrific bed-and-breakfast, Josephine's. You can walk leisurely from one end of town to the other in less than half an hour. Seaside's focal point, the town square, has an amphitheater, restaurants, shops, and galleries. Across County Road 30A from the square on the beach side there are more restaurants and boutiques.

Cottages at Seaside

On the beach side of the road, you'll find Seaside's open-air market-place atop the dunes. Here are beach shops, like Sue Vaneer's and Ono Surf Shop, and walk-up eateries, like Pickles, Roly Poly, Café Spiazzia, and Hurricane Oyster Bar. You'll also find Bud & Alley's, an outstanding restaurant with entrées that include Black Iron-Seared Sea Scallops with Asiago Cheese Grits and Tomato Basil Pan Sauce, and Blue Crab Cakes on Balsamic Greens with Roasted Pecans and Lemon Butter. My favorite (which sounds like a heart attack waiting to happen) is the Carpet Bag Steak: wood-grilled tenderloin stuffed with Apalachicola fried oysters, smothered in béarnaise, and served with spinach-and-herb mashed potatoes. By the way, Bud was the owner's dachshund, and Alley was Bud's friend, a beach cat.

The nine beach pavilions serve as passageways to the Gulf. These are Seaside's icons. Open framework, lattice, arches, a hint of Art Deco—each pavilion has its own personality and style. My favorite is the West Ruskin Street Pavilion, designed by Michael McDonough. Facing the highway side, it has a tall, pyramid-shaped, wood-frame extension of the roof gable. Each of the sixteen squares in the frame contains a sail-boat likeness. From this elevated spot atop the scrub-covered dunes, you

East Ruskin Street Pavilion

have a commanding view of the Gulf shore. Follow the boardwalk down onto the beach, which, along with Grayton Beach State Recreational Area one mile west of here, is consistently rated among the finest beaches in the world. The unusually bright, white sand contrasts with the vivid, emerald Gulf water that gives this coast its name. The sand consists of fine, powdered quartz washed down from the Appalachian Mountains over the eons. It's like walking on powdered sugar.

Back across the road around Central Square are more eateries, galleries, and shops, among them Sundog Books. Sundog has a great selection of books on Florida, nature, and architecture, but they are best stocked with "beach books," mystery and romance novels. There's also a terrific grocery/delicatessen market, the Modica Market, with fifteen-foot-high shelves of gourmet goods requiring rolling library ladders to reach their tops. And don't miss the tiny Bow Wow Meow, which describes itself as a shop "for dogs, cats, and their humans."

This was Robert Davis's vision. Inspired by his childhood memories of summers spent in beach cottages on this coast, he built a town from scratch. Davis went to architects Andres Duany and Elizabeth Plater-Zyberk at Arquitectonica in Miami to help plan the layout of Seaside and to draw up the town's building code. Seaside's first houses went up in 1982. Since then, the architectural world has praised it as a community that blends function, beauty, and a definitive sense of place like no other.

The first time I visited Seaside, in 1996, it was still somewhat isolated—off the beaten path. In the years since then, scores of imitators have popped up around it, namely, Rosemary Beach to the east and several developments on Santa Rosa Beach to the west. The newest is an Arvida development called Watercolor, immediately next door to Seaside. County Road 30A has changed from "*Off* the beaten path" to "It *is* the beaten path." Of course, it was Seaside that spawned this explosion, and the others attempt to copy Seaside's architecture, but none have been able to reproduce its charm and magic. There's nothing like the original.

Seaside is a holiday town from the past that has been heralded as a model community for the future. It is one of the original and best examples of New Urbanism. Sometimes called Neo-traditional Town Planning or Traditional Neighborhood Design, New Urbanism is a community design concept that attempts to maximize the interaction of neighbors, to minimize automobile use, and to place a town's (or neighborhood's) living quarters within walking distance of its commercial center. "New" is somewhat of a misnomer. The concept is based largely on old, good ideas and a return to pre–World War II (read: pre–suburban sprawl) neighborhoods and towns. Front porches, small picket-fenced front yards, and sidewalks all encourage getting to know your neighbors. It's a concept I like, as long as it is implemented in a way that embraces the local culture, history, and character. Seaside does that beautifully.

DIRECTIONS: Take Highway 98 west of Panama City to CR 30A.

DON'T MISS: Bud & Alley's Restaurant
ADDRESSES AND EVENTS: see page 191-192

CARRABELLE, ST. GEORGE ISLAND,
AND
APALACHICOLA

*Population: Carrabelle 1,303; St. George Island
500 (estimated); Apalachicola 2,334*

FROM PANACEA TO APALACHICOLA, HIGHWAY 98 follows what Panhandlers call the Forgotten Coast. I can see why they call this coast "forgotten." There's seldom any traffic on the highway and only a few houses, most built high up on telephone-pole stilts. Pine forest grows right up to the water's edge.

Somewhere near the center of the Forgotten Coast, you'll pass through the town of **Carrabelle**. Carrabelle grew up around the mouth

On the beach at St. George Island

27

Carrabelle Police Station

of the Carrabelle River. In the late 1800s, it was a lumber-shipping town with several large sawmills. Now it's a sport and commercial fishing community that can claim the World's Smallest Police Station, a phone booth in the middle of town.

Just over the Carrabelle River Bridge from town, on the left, is Julia Mae's World Famous Seafood Restaurant. The obligatory giant grouper dominates the sign. The parking lot is packed—more pickup trucks than cars. Predictable fish-house decor graces the interior: sea life taxidermy, nets, an old Coast Guard life preserver, and some fishing tournament trophies. The menu offers just about everything that swims—fried, broiled, or grilled. I like the "small" seafood platter—piled high with fried shrimp, scallops, oysters, grouper, and some of the best blue-crab fingers I've tasted. I've never been able to finish half of it (perhaps if they offered a child's plate).

Continue east through Eastpoint, and then turn south on Route 300 and cross the four-mile-long causeway to **St. George Island.** My sister-in-law Kelly Hunt told me about St. George. Kelly grew up in

Tallahassee and often vacationed on the island.

St. George Island is a thirty-mile-long permanent sandbar. Blinding white beaches, sand dunes, sea oats, and more telephone-pole stilt houses characterize the scenery. Pristine Julian G. Bruce/St. George Island State Park occupies the eastern tip of the island. Seclusion is the main attraction here. Most visitors rent one of the beach houses by the week or the month. Don't come looking for a lot of excitement or nightlife here. This is more of a sit-in-a-beach-chair-and-read-a-paperback kind of place. Besides peace and quiet, another of St. George's attractions is the dog-friendly beach.

Continue west on Highway 98 to **Apalachicola**, the Oyster Capital. Apalachicola sits on the end of the elbow in the Panhandle where the Apalachicola River joins the Gulf of Mexico. Its history has seesawed between booms and economic droughts. In the 1820s, this was a big cotton-shipping port. Cotton warehouses went up along the river in 1838, and in 1839, Florida's first railroad was built from here to St. Joseph (now Port St. Joe) to the west. That railroad didn't last, though. In 1841, the people of St. Joseph were decimated by an outbreak of yellow fever. In 1844, the town was flooded by a hurricane. Twenty years later, new railroads rerouted trade east and west, and for a while Apalachicola lost its importance as a port. But in the 1880s, cypress milling revitalized the town. Then, in the 1920s, it became the center of Florida's booming seafood industry. Apalachicola is, to this day, best known for its oysters.

Since the mid-1980s, another kind of revitalization has taken place— the restoration of Apalachicola's historic homes and buildings. Cross the Apalachicola River Bridge and the first building you'll see, the Gibson Inn, was the first to be restored.

The Gibson Inn (see photo page 27) is now the centerpiece of Apalachicola's historic district. When the National Trust for Historic Preservation published its coffee-table book, *America Restored*, the Gibson Inn was one of the two Florida buildings featured. The three-story, Victorian-style hotel is blue and gray with white trim. A cupola and widow's walk crown its tin roof. Wide first- and second-floor verandas wrap around three of its sides. Wooden rockers and Adirondack chairs on the verandas invite the inn's guests to "set a spell," have a cup of coffee, read a book, or maybe just scratch behind the ears of one of the four resident cats.

The Gibson Inn was called the Franklin Inn when it opened in 1907. The name changed in 1923 when the Gibson sisters bought it. These were grand years at the inn, but the opulence of that era declined with the passing decades. The inn had been boarded up for some time when, in 1983, Michael Koun, his brother Neal, and some investing friends bought the hotel for $90,000. Over the next two years, they spent $1 million meticulously rebuilding and restoring it to its original, turn-of-the-century grandeur. Their best architectural reference was a collection of old photos taken in 1910. The photographer had spent that year photographing Apalachicola and the surrounding area. Now, a number of his pictures hang on the walls in the Gibson Inn's dining room.

Four-poster beds and period antiques fill each of the Gibson Inn's thirty-one guest rooms. Wooden-slat blinds decorate the windows. Artisans built the lobby staircase from scratch, using a single surviving newel post as their guide. Rich cypress is used throughout the inn. My favorite room, the bar, has a grand, nautical feel, as though it should have been on the *Titanic*. Just two weeks after the Gibson reopened in November 1985, Hurricane Kate slammed the central Panhandle. The Kouns kept the bar open and threw a Key Largo–style hurricane party. Humphrey Bogart would have approved.

I met Michael Koun on my first visit to Apalachicola. He is a tall, soft-spoken gentleman, and his love for Apalachicola showed from the minute we began to talk. Before long he had convinced me to ride with him while he "did a few errands." Actually what he did was take me on a tour of the town.

From the inn, we drove west a few blocks and crisscrossed through the district of lumber baron homes. "Silk stockings district," Michael called it. It's a magnificent neighborhood of Edwardian and Victorian homes. Nearly all of them have been or are in the process of being restored. Many wealthy, textile people, and later lumber people, owned homes here, and Michael knew the background on all of them. Two of the most impressive homes were the John Ruge House at Avenue B and Eleventh Street, and the Willis House, overlooking the bay on Bay Avenue. The house of John Ruge, one of the lumber barons, is yellow with bright red trim and has a widow's walk, a much-repeated architectural motif in Apalachicola. The Willis House is white with a wrap-

Ruge House on Bay Avenue, Apalachicola

Willis House on Bay Avenue, Apalachicola

around porch, a tin roof, and a white picket fence around the front yard. Michael pointed out, "The tin roofs reflect heat, the porches cool the air around the house, and the windows let the air flow through. These larger, more palatial homes came in the eighteen eighties with the lumber boom. Most of the smaller homes built in the cotton-shipping days are about forty years older than that."

Around the corner, Michael stopped to exchange hellos with a woman working in her garden. "People have moved here from all corners of the country," he explained as we pulled away. "Apalachicola has been rediscovered, become a town that people want to live in. This is a working town, not a retirement town. We want people to come here and enjoy it, but we don't want it to become a tourist town. It's unique in that it has this beautiful historic area, it's in a beautiful geographical and environmental area, and people want to come see these things. But we're a working community first, with families and year-round residents." Five thousand people populated Apalachicola 150 years ago; only three thousand live here today.

As we crisscrossed the various lettered avenues and numbered streets, Michael explained the town's layout. "The land that Apalachicola sits on was originally part of the Forbes Purchase; then it was sold to the Apalachicola Land Company. This was a company town. The city was laid out using the plat of Philadelphia, with town squares every four or five blocks. The idea was that the squares would be small centers of business. That never happened. All the business went up on the waterfront, but the residential section still has these small town squares every few blocks."

I don't think Michael finished any of his errands, because he spent the remainder of the afternoon showing me Apalachicola and telling me about its history. We saw the Trinity Episcopal Church on 6th Street, which was actually shipped in pieces from New York and reassembled here in 1837. We visited the Chestnut Street Cemetery, where gravestones show birth dates as far back as the 1770s. At Avenue D and 5th Street, he showed me the Myers-Macy House, a steamboat-style house that was a headquarters for the Confederacy during the Civil War. I could not have asked for a better tour guide.

The Apalachicola River has been the town's lifeblood for its entire existence. In the early 1800s, cotton was the main product that traversed the river. From the 1860s to 1880s, sponge fishing was big here.

Many Greek sponge fishermen came to Apalachicola before ultimately settling in Tarpon Springs. In the late 1800s, cypress and pine were shipped along the river. Water Street, on the east side of downtown, runs along the waterfront. City Hall, at Avenue E and Water Street, was originally a cotton warehouse that was built in 1838. One thing that visitors notice about downtown is how wide the streets are. That's because back in the cotton-shipping days, cotton was unloaded at the docks and then had to be stacked on the streets where it could be compressed before being moved into the warehouses.

Of course, shrimping and oystering have been and are still big industries in Apalachicola. Packinghouses line both ends of Water Street, and shrimp and oyster boats fill the docks. There are some interesting historical buildings in this district. Apalachicola native John Grady opened his ship chandlery business in 1884 to service cargo ships and the lumber-shipping industry. The red-brick J. E. Grady and Company Building at 76 Water Street was built in 1900 to replace a wooden building destroyed by a fire that consumed many of the buildings on the waterfront earlier that year. Current owners Herbert and Virginia Dugger spent three years on a meticulous restoration and reopened the building in 1998. The Grady Market, a clothing, art, and antiques store, occupies the downstairs. Upstairs, The Consulate Suites offers four luxury suites to visitors. Three blocks north you'll find Wefing's Marine and Nautical Supply, a fascinating place to walk through. Wefing's sells everything for boats and commercial fishing—charts, nets, hardware, and motor parts—and has been here since 1909.

There's no shortage of excellent food in Apalachicola. At the far south end of Water Street is the famous Boss Oyster Restaurant, where the specialty is oysters, prepared sixteen different ways. Try Tamara's Floridita Café on Avenue E. Tamara came to Apalachicola from Caracas, Venezuela, and brought many wonderful recipes from her home country. Another favorite of mine is the Owl Café, at Avenue D and Commerce Street. Greek brothers John and Constantine Nichols opened their restaurant and boardinghouse here in 1908. Back then the specialty of the house was "whole loaf," a hollowed-out loaf of bread filled with oysters and a variety of sauces, then baked. Today the Owl Café's menu changes daily, but expect marvelous entrées like Black Grouper Fillet, sautéed with artichoke hearts, capers, roast garlic, and lemon, or Filet Mignon with Gorgonzola Cream Sauce.

Michael had recommended that I go to the John Gorrie State Museum on 6th Street, and I found that the museum told one of Apalachicola's most interesting stories. John Gorrie was a physician who came to Apalachicola in 1833. He became a driving force in the community and served as mayor, postmaster, and city treasurer. He founded the aforementioned Trinity Episcopal Church. His most significant contribution, however, was his invention of the ice machine.

Dr. Gorrie treated yellow fever victims during the epidemic of 1841. He was convinced that by cooling them down they would have a better chance of recovering. In 1842, he began working on a design for a device that would lower the temperature of the air. By 1844, he had constructed a machine that, more or less, cooled air by removing heat through the rapid expansion of gases (the same basic principle used in air conditioners and refrigerators today). A byproduct of the functioning of the machine was that it made bricks of ice, and ice-making turned out to be its most important asset. In 1851, Dr. Gorrie received a U.S. patent for his invention.

The museum chronicles John Gorrie's remarkable life and accomplishments. On display is a replica of his ice machine, built according to the plans in his patent. The sad ending to Dr. Gorrie's tale is that until his death in 1855, he worked hard to market the machine but was completely unsuccessful. He died never knowing the enormous impact his invention would have on the world.

DIRECTIONS: Carrabelle is 60 miles southwest of Tallahassee on Highway 98/319 on the coast. From Carrabelle, continue west along the coast to Eastpoint. Turn south across the toll bridge, Highway G1A/300, to St. George Island. From Eastpoint, drive west on Highway 98/319 across the bridge into Apalachicola.

DON'T MISS: The Gibson Inn in Apalachicola
ADDRESSES AND EVENTS: see page 192–193

WAKULLA SPRINGS

Population: 100 (estimated)

"CENTURIES OF PASSION PENT UP IN HIS SAVAGE HEART!" is the tag line on the movie posters for Universal Studio's 1954 sci-fi/horror classic *The Creature from the Black Lagoon*. Archaeologists, played by Richard Carlson and Julie Adams, discover the prehistoric gill-man/monster, played by Ben Chapman, while on an expedition deep in the Amazon. Filmed mostly underwater in 3-D, the film was a technological, special-effects marvel in its day. Universal chose Wakulla Springs, fifteen miles south of Tallahassee, as the film's location because of its exceptionally clear waters.

Wakulla Springs, part of Edward Ball Wakulla Springs State Park, is the largest and deepest spring in the world. Its waters are so clear that details at the bottom, 185 feet deep, are easily discernible from the surface. It actually has been the site of numerous archaeological excavations. In 1935, divers discovered a complete mastodon skeleton at the bottom of the springs. The reconstructed mastodon now stands in the Museum of Florida History in the R. A. Gray Building at the Capitol in Tallahassee.

The springs had its own recently living, prehistoric creature too—although by all accounts it was not a malevolent one. Old Joe was a 650-pound, 11-foot-2-inch alligator that had been seen at the springs since the 1920s. Although he had never shown aggressive behavior, Old Joe was shot and killed by an unknown assailant in August 1966, when the alligator was estimated to be two hundred years old. Carl Buchheister, then-president of the Audubon Society, offered a $5,000 reward for information leading to the arrest of the gunman, but no one was ever charged with killing Old Joe.

The 185-foot-deep Wakulla Springs, where 1954 sci-fi/horror classic The Creature from the Black Lagoon *and numerous* Tarzan *features were filmed.*

All manner of wildlife thrives in the park. In addition to alligators, deer, raccoons, and even a few bears live here. Bird watchers can spot a variety of winged creatures, including anhingas, purple gallinules, herons, egrets, ospreys, and long-billed limpkins (called "crying birds" because of their shrieking, almost-humanlike cry). On my first visit to the park, when I passed through the entrance gate, the ranger warned me to be cautious if I hiked the trail down to the Sally Ward Spring. "Where you see the red ribbons," she told me, "that marks the area where one of our momma gators is keeping close watch over her new brood of babies. Needless to say, she's being very protective." I assured the park ranger that I would heed her advice.

Edward Ball was the brother-in-law of Alfred I. DuPont. He was also the executor and trustee of DuPont's sizable estate and trust. Ball built a banking, telephone, railroad, and paper-and-box manufacturing empire out of the DuPont trust. DuPont's estate was worth an estimated $33 million when he died in 1935. Ball had grown that into more than $2 billion by the time he passed away in 1981 at the age of ninety-three.

One of Edward Ball's proudest achievements was the construction of the Wakulla Springs Lodge in 1937. The twenty-seven-room lodge is essentially the same today as it was in the 1930s. Ball insisted that it always continue to reflect that era and also that it never become so exclusive that it would not be affordable to "common folks." I visited the lodge and the springs on a sunny fall morning. Wakulla Springs Lodge reminded me of a palatial Spanish hacienda. The first thing that caught my eye when I walked into the lobby were the cypress ceiling beams with hand-painted crests and scenes of Florida. Blue and gold Spanish tiles frame the entranceway. The floors are mauve, red, and gray Tennessee marble tiles in a checkerboard pattern. A giant fireplace, made from native limestone and trimmed in marble, dominates the far wall.

A long glass case at one end of the lobby contains the stuffed and mounted remains of Old Joe. His plaque reads, "Old Joe's first and only cage." The most interesting room in the lodge is just past Old Joe's case—the soda fountain shop. There is no bar in the Wakulla Springs Lodge. Instead, Ball, who was fond of ginger whips (ice cream, ginger ale, and whipped cream), had a sixty-foot-long solid marble soda fountain counter installed.

After having a steaming bowl of navy bean soup for lunch (one of the dining room's specialties), I walked down to the springs. From the top of a twenty-foot-high diving platform, I looked down on bream and bass schooling on the bottom. The water is amazingly clear: it's like looking through glass. It's no wonder that Hollywood came to this location to film Tarzan features and movies like *Around the World Under the Sea*, *Airport 77*, and *The Creature from the Black Lagoon*.

Wakulla Springs State Park is as serene a setting as you could hope to find. Nature trails leading out from the lodge take hikers through hardwood forest and past sinkholes and springs. The lodge also operates glass-bottom boat tours.

DIRECTIONS: Take SR 61 south from Tallahassee and go east on SR 267.

DON'T MISS: Old Joe
ADDRESSES AND EVENTS: see page 193

ST. MARKS AND SOPCHOPPY

*Population: St. Marks 272;
Sopchoppy 426*

WHICH CAME FIRST, STATE ROAD 363 OR POSEY'S OYSTER BAR in St. Marks? I'm not sure, but if the oyster bar predates the highway, which runs straight south from the Capitol for twenty miles, then dead-ends a half block from Posey's, then my guess is that some shellfish-loving legislators had something to do with the road's construction.

St. Marks sits at the confluence of the Wakulla and St. Marks Rivers. The two combined waterways then flow another three miles south into the Gulf of Mexico. This has been a strategic location for lots of different people throughout history. It was an important village for the Apalachee Indians in 1528, when Spanish explorer Panfilo de Narváez ran into them on his trek toward Mexico. The Apalachees gave him and his men such a scare that they hastily built rafts and took to the sea for the remainder of their journey. (Narváez and most of his crew drowned during violent storms on the Gulf before reaching Mexico.) In the early 1600s, Spanish missionaries built the Mission San Marcos de Apalache (hence the name St. Marks) because they felt it was important to convert the Indians to Christianity. In 1680, Spanish troops thought that the location had strategic military importance and built the wooden

Fort San Marcos de Apalache. Over the next two hundred years, the fort was alternately rebuilt and occupied by Spanish, French, British, and eventually American troops, the last in 1819, when General Andrew Jackson seized the fort following the conclusion of the First Seminole War. Some remains of the fort can still be seen at its site just off State Road 363.

The town of St. Marks was incorporated in 1830, and it became an important shipping port. The Tallahassee Railroad Company built one of the state's first railroads, from Tallahassee to St. Marks, in 1837. Mules pulled the cars. Today that route has been converted into the sixteen-mile Tallahassee–St. Marks Historic Trail, a Rails-to-Trails project.

In 1929, Birdie Coggins convinced her husband, Steve, and friend T. J. Posey that the three of them should open a riverfront restaurant in St. Marks. They called it the City Café, and it gained rapid fame as the best seafood joint in this part of the state. Tallahassee politicians, including a succession of governors, were regular customers. Important deals were made over baskets of fried fish and Birdie's famous, secret-recipe hush puppies.

The City Café closed in the late 1940s, but T. J. Posey reopened it a few years later as Posey's Oyster Bar. Posey was an important man in St. Marks. He was a member of the Wakulla County Commission and St. Marks City Council, and he served as a judge and eventually as mayor. A year after Steve Coggins passed away in 1965, Birdie married Posey and was back in the restaurant business for a while. Sometime around 1970, carnival operator Bill Helson bought Posey's and kept the good name. In 1989, Walter and Nancy Beckham, along with Walter's brother Donny, bought it from Helson. In 2003, Daphne Beckham, Donny's daughter, began taking over operation of the restaurant.

Posey's Oyster Bar, a white two-story, wood-frame building with green trim, backs up to the St. Marks River. From the front it looks identical to photographs taken of it in the 1930s when it was the City Café. The only difference I can see is that the signs now read "Posey's Famous Smoked Mullet" and "Home of Posey's Topless Oysters." It's still a seafood restaurant (although you can get chicken or a burger or a corn dog, if you insist), and it's still famous. Naturally oysters are the specialty, and you can have them in any combination: raw or baked with butter, garlic, cheddar cheese, parmesan cheese, bacon, and, of course, cocktail sauce, horseradish, and lemon.

Florida State University students pack Posey's on the weekends, when live bands play, and it's a popular place with the Tallahassee political set. Burt Reynolds, an FSU graduate, is a frequent customer—and sometimes Jerry Reed comes with him. A poster tacked up across from the bar contains a long list of other celebrities and dignitaries who have dined at Posey's, among them George and Barbara Bush and Princess Caroline.

Eating oysters and going fishing are the two main reasons people come to St. Marks, but there is more to see. The St. Marks National Wildlife Refuge, just four miles east (go back up to Highway 98, then take State Road 59 south), is home to a wide variety of coastal woodlands wildlife—everything from anhingas to alligators. The St. Marks Lighthouse, at the south end of State Road 59 in the Wildlife Refuge, was built in 1829. The eighty-foot-tall, stucco-over-brick structure had to be moved back from the encroaching sea in 1841. Confederate troops were stationed here during the Civil War.

It's tough to resist detouring up County Road 319, off Highway 98, just to pass through the town of **Sopchoppy.** The name is likely a mispronunciation of two Creek Indian words that describe the river that flows past the town: *sokhe* and *chapke*, meaning "twisted" and "long." Or, the Creek Indians might have been describing something else—worms. Worms have put Sopchoppy on the map. The variety that breeds in this area's soil is particularly fat and long—a fisherman's dream. The method used to bring them to the surface is called grunting (or gruntin'). The worm grunter's tools are a wooden stake and a flattened iron paddle. Something amazing happens when a grunter drives a stake into the ground and grinds the iron paddle against it: worms come wriggling out of the ground by the hundreds. The grunting noise that the grinding makes sends a vibration through the ground that makes the little slimy guys crazy. On the second weekend in April, Sopchoppy holds its annual Worm Gruntin' Festival and Worm Grunter's Ball. There's lots of good food and live entertainment; they choose a Worm Queen; and the highlight is, of course, the Worm Gruntin' Contest to see who can grunt up the most worms in fifteen minutes. In 1972, Charles Kuralt brought worm grunting to the attention of the outside world, much to the chagrin of locals. Following that publicity, the U. S. Forest Service began requiring a permit and charging fees for grunting.

Sopchoppy has a grocery store, a hardware store, and a bait and tackle shop. There are also a couple of restaurants, including a combination pizza joint and outfitters shop called Backwoods Pizza/Sopchoppy Outfitters, located in a restored 1912 pharmacy building.

DIRECTIONS: Take SR 363 south from Tallahassee until it ends.

DON'T MISS: Posey's Oyster Bar. Don't worry—you can't miss it.
ADDRESSES AND EVENTS: see page 193–194

JASPER

Population: 1,780

MOST SMALL TOWNS HAVE A GATHERING PLACE, the kind of place where, if you fail to check in with established regularity, folks begin to wonder if you've taken ill or something: "Old Henry hasn't come in for breakfast in a coupla days. Wonder if he's taken to feeling poorly?" The kind of place where, if you're an out-of-towner who has stopped in while passing through, the regulars will have learned the better part of your life story before you leave—and you'll have learned a good bit of theirs.

The H & F Restaurant in Jasper is one of those places. It's open seven days a week, breakfast and lunch only. There's no menu; it's always a buffet. I first heard about it from my friend Margaret Hartley. "There's this great little Southern diner in Jasper. . . ."

Say no more.

My travel companion, Loretta Jordan, and I walked in around 11:15 Sunday morning just ahead of the church crowd. I commented on how good the vegetables looked, and a gentleman in the buffet line ahead of us turned and asked politely, "Ya'll's first time here?" And a conversation commenced.

It's not just the vegetables that looked tasty. Everything on the buffet stirred my appetite. The ancestors of most of the long-time locals in Jasper—like those in nearly every small north Florida town—are from Georgia, Alabama, and South Carolina. The food here reflects that heritage: fried chicken, sausage, roast beef and gravy, turnip greens (with lots of ham hock), yellow squash, fresh pole beans, okra and tomato, butter beans, cornbread dressing (my favorite), and dessert (bread pudding and three kinds of cake: strawberry, pineapple, and coconut).

"H and F is Handy and Frana. That's my mom and dad," owner Maureen Riley told me. "They started the place. Been at this same location since nineteen sixty-eight. Having it all-buffet makes it easier to operate, plus folks can better choose what they want to eat when they're looking right at it. There's a hunting reserve near here, so we get lots of hunters in here during the season from all over north Florida and south Georgia. Then there're the regulars we get in here day in and day out. They're all like family."

We sat down at one of the family-style tables with our heaping plates. "Where ya'll from?" someone asked. And a conversation commenced.

DIRECTIONS: Take Hamilton CR 6 (Exit 460) east from I-75.

DON'T MISS: The cornbread dressing at the H & F Restaurant
ADDRESSES AND EVENTS: see page 194

WHITE SPRINGS

Population: 819

IN 1935, THE FLORIDA STATE LEGISLATURE CHOSE Stephen Foster's melody "Old Folks at Home," better known as "Way Down Upon the Suwannee River," as the official state song. Ironically, Foster never once set foot in the state of Florida, much less on the banks of the Suwannee. (It's likely that, except for a single trip to New Orleans, Foster never ventured south of Cincinnati, Ohio.) In his original draft of the song, which was ultimately published in 1851, he had written, "Way down upon the Pee Dee River," but it just didn't ring true for him. (The Pee Dee River is in South Carolina, and he had never been there either.) With the aid of an atlas and the assistance of his brother, Morrison, Stephen tried inserting a variety of river names into his song, including Yazoo. None sounded right until he hit on Suwannee.

Born on July 4, 1826, and raised in Lawrenceville, Pennsylvania, Stephen Foster was one of the first composers to adopt a purely American style. Some of his most famous songs are "Oh! Susanna," "My Old Kentucky Home" (declared Kentucky's official state song in 1928), "Old Black Joe," "Jeanie with the Light Brown Hair," "Beautiful Dreamer," and "Camptown Races." Many of Foster's songs depicted the lifestyles, longings, and concerns of black slaves in the Deep South, and he wrote his lyrics in a dialect that reflected the way the slaves spoke. "Way Down Upon the Suwannee River" was actually written, "Way Down Upon de Swanee Ribber." In later years, some interpreted his style as degrading; in reality, the opposite was true. Foster was very sympathetic to the slaves' plight. His songs and the style in which he wrote them lent legitimacy to their situation.

Tragically, the last years of Stephen Foster's life were depressing. Despite his success as a song composer, he was broke. His marriage had failed, and he was an alcoholic. He died when he was only thirty-seven in 1864 from complications following a bad fall. Like so many others, his genius was not truly appreciated until years after he was gone.

There are three major memorials to Stephen Foster. One is at the University of Pittsburgh near his hometown. Another is in Bardstown, Kentucky. The third, the Stephen Foster Memorial and Folk Culture Center, is in White Springs, Florida, alongside the Suwannee River. It opened in 1950, ninety-nine years after "Way Down Upon the Suwannee River" was first published.

In the 1700s, White Sulpher Spring was sacred ground to the local Indians. They felt that the spring, which spills into the Suwannee, had special curative powers. Indian warriors wounded in battle were not attacked when they came to the springs to recuperate. After settlers moved here in the early 1800s, word of the water's medicinal properties spread. Eventually, developers built a posh health resort and spa around the springs. Teddy Roosevelt was a regular visitor.

Today, there are few remaining signs of White Springs' resort days, although there are some magnificent, antebellum homes. Of the original dozen or so hotels, the only one still standing is the 1903 Telford Hotel, a copper-roofed, three-story, brick-and-stone structure in the center of town. In its day, the Telford hosted Presidents Taft and Roosevelt, J. P. Morgan, John D. Rockefeller, George Firestone, and Thomas Edison. Currently, a portion of the hotel is being used as a radio broadcast studio for the nationally syndicated radio program "For the People."

The Highway 136 bridge crosses a deep (for Florida) gorge carved by the Suwannee River. On just the other side of the bridge, Highway 136 intersects Highway 41, and this is the heart of the tiny community of White Springs. Immediately on the left is White Spring's new Nature & Heritage Tourism Center, operated by the Florida State Park Service. Make this your first stop: it's a terrific source for books and maps, as well as information for canoe outfitters and festival-goers.

Across the street is American Canoe Adventures, which rents and sells canoes and kayaks, as well as organizes trips on the Suwannee.

Increasingly, year-round visitors are enjoying the beauty of the river from the vantage point of a canoe or kayak.

A quarter of a mile north of the intersection on Highway 41 is the entrance to the Stephen Foster State Folk Culture Center, a 250-acre park and memorial to the songwriter. Your first stop should be the Stephen Foster Museum, housed in a large, Southern plantation house with six giant, two-story, white columns on its front porch. The north wing has a collection of old, unusual, and ornate pianos. One of the most interesting is an 1875 Steinway duplex scale piano with six tiered rows of keys. Another is a small, upright Frederick Haupt/Leipzig that Stephen Foster had played regularly at the home of one of his neighbors in Pittsburgh. Morrison Foster's fold-out office desk and chair sit against one wall. A plaque describes the desk as the one that Morrison and Stephen sat at while studying the atlas for an appropriate river name for "Old Folks at Home." The center hall contains dioramas that portray scenes described in Foster's most popular songs. In the south wing there are more pianos and a ten-foot-tall Howard Chandler Christy painting of Stephen Foster done in 1948.

The centerpiece of the park is the ninety-seven-bell carillon in the top of a two-hundred-foot-tall, brick bell tower built in 1958. The bells are of a tubular construction rather than of the more conventional cast type. The carillon plays a program of Stephen Foster tunes on an electronic music roll similar to a player piano's, and sometimes guest carillonneurs play. Across from the bell tower, in the Craft Square, artisans demonstrate their various, centuries-old crafting skills like blacksmithing and wood carving. The Stephen Foster State Folk Culture Center holds special events throughout the year, but the biggest event is the annual Florida Folk Festival, one of the most popular folk music festivals in the country.

Near the park entrance, a wooden walkway leads to the banks of the Suwannee. The gorge is at least one hundred feet deep. The river flows past at a fairly good clip. Limestone boulders hold up the bank on this side. Tall cypress trees, thick with moss, lean out over the water. If you squint, you can almost see Seminole Indians walking a trail on the other side.

The name Suwannee has two possible sources. In the 1700s, the river was called the Little San Juan, in acknowledgment of the San Juan De Guacara Mission located on its banks. Local dialect may have corrupted

San Juan into San wanee. The more likely possibility is that the name is derived from the Creek Indian word *suwani*, which means "echo." This makes sense, because the steep walls of the gorge formed by the river do create a good echo.

DIRECTIONS: Take I-75 to the Highway 136/White Springs exit (Exit 439). Go east.

DON'T MISS: Stephen Foster State Folk Culture Center
ADDRESSES AND EVENTS: see page 194

KEATON BEACH, DEKLE BEACH, AND ADAMS BEACH

Population: Keaton Beach 300 (estimated); Dekle Beach 200 (estimated); Adams Beach 0

IN THE VERY EARLY MORNING HOURS OF MARCH 13, 1993, the third most devastating storm ever to hit the continental United States made land-fall on the north end of Florida's Big Bend area. Its strongest winds struck the tiny coastal communities of Dekle Beach and Keaton Beach, where ten people were killed and 150 homes were severely damaged or destroyed (only two houses in Dekle Beach were left unscathed). The total loss for the entire state of Florida would end up at twenty-six lives, eighteen thousand homes, and more than $500 million in property damage. Over the next couple of days, the storm would continue across the state and all the way up the East Coast, turning into a horrific blizzard. Because the storm hadn't formed as a traditional hurricane does, it wasn't given a name, despite record storm surges and winds well over one hundred miles per hour. Most simply remember it as the "No Name Storm of 1993." Those who experienced it refer to it as "The Storm of the Century."

Just south of Perry, Highway 361 carves a narrow path west and then south through unpopulated pine forest and eventually cypress marsh as it approaches the coast. This is not "coast" in the conventional Florida sense. There are no natural beaches. The woods and wetlands grow right up to the edge of the usually calm waters of the Gulf of Mexico. They call this the Nature Coast. On the map, Keaton, Dekle, and Adams Beaches appear as three little dots in a row on Taylor County's coast. **Adams** is the northernmost of the three. In the 1860s, it was called Jonesville, and there was a salt collection and processing plant here that supplied Confederate troops during the Civil War. Now it is simply the place where a spur road off Highway 361 (Adams Beach Road) dead-ends at the Gulf. You can look both up and down the coast and not see a single sign of human intervention. It is strikingly majestic. This is probably pretty close to what it looked like to the Timucuan Indians, the original inhabitants of this region.

A few miles south of Adams, you'll find **Dekle Beach**, where one fishing pier and several docks occupy the shoreline and three or four dozen homes sit atop towering stilts. It looks like they had a contest to see who could build the tallest stilt house. Most of them are thirty or forty feet above the ground.

A few more miles south of Dekle is **Keaton Beach,** which is a little larger than Dekle Beach. Keaton Beach sits on property originally owned by a sawmill and turpentine businessman named Captain Brown back in the mid-1800s. Brown liked his bookkeeper, Sam Keaton, so much that he named the little community after him. Keaton Beach has a motel, a small marina, Hodges Park on the tiny man-made beach, and the Keaton Beach Hot Dog Stand right across from the park.

The Keaton Beach Hot Dog Stand is "the hot dog stand at the edge of the world." It seems such an anomaly, way out here. A gargantuan, menacing-looking shark's head hangs outside over its entrance. Inside it's a cozy eatery with picnic tables and benches, where, in addition to

Keaton Beach Hot Dog Stand—the hot dog stand at the edge of the world.

hot dogs, you can get burgers, chicken, and fresh seafood. The hot dog stand has been here since the mid-1970s. It was called Ruth's originally. Martha and Bill Hargeshiemer bought it in 1985 when they moved up to Keaton Beach from Plant City. In 2001, Ron Wheeler, a paramedic from Ohio, bought it from the Hargeshiemers. The first time I visited Keaton Beach, I spoke to Martha and Bill Hargeshiemer about the storm.

"Well, we had a roof left," Bill told me, "but that was it."

Martha pulled three photo albums out from under the counter and passed them over to me. "I was here when it hit. Bill was down in Tampa. Around six o'clock on the twelfth [March 12, 1993], I called the Coast Guard station down at Horseshoe Beach—they are about thirty-five miles south of here—and asked, 'Is it getting bad?' We have a lot of commercial fishermen in this area, so weather is a constant concern. The Coast Guard station tells me, 'Maybe sixty-mile-per-hour winds and two-to-four-foot seas.' Nobody knew what was coming. It hit like a freight train around three-thirty in the morning [March 13]. We had one-hundred-ten- to one-hundred-twenty-five-mile-per-hour winds. The storm surge brought flood waters eight to ten feet high here—it pushed water inland all the way up to the curve in the road (about a quarter mile in). Houses floated up off their foundations. At Dekle it reached as high as seventeen feet. That's why all their new houses are built up so high. It continued to blow until about eight o'clock in the morning. Rescue crews spent the next two days removing bodies from the tops of trees over in Dekle."

I thumbed through Martha's photo albums, looking at before-and-after photos of houses and buildings and reading newspaper accounts of the havoc dispensed by the storm. Perhaps to change the subject to something more light, Martha asked if I would sign their guest book. It contained more than three thousand signatures and hometowns. Travelers from as far away as South Africa, Italy, Norway, and Great Britain have signed the book. Former President Jimmy Carter, his family, and his bodyguards all signed it in December 1994 while on their way to Steinhatchee for Christmas.

Across the parking lot is Hodges Park on the beach, where a commemorative plaque dedicates the park to the memory of those who died in the storm and to those who survived. Reading the plaque is sobering: it lists the names and ages of the Taylor County residents who died. Four were children. Whole families were wiped out.

Keaton Beach and Dekle Beach have long since rebuilt, but the memory of March 13, 1993, will stay forever with their residents.

DIRECTIONS: Take SR 361 southwest from US Highway 19 south of Perry.

DON'T MISS: Keaton Beach Hot Dog Stand
ADDRESSES AND EVENTS: see page 194

STEINHATCHEE

Population: 200 (estimated)

THAT'S *STEEN*-HAT-CHEE. AT LEAST THAT'S THE WAY THE LOCALS SAY IT. It's their town; therefore, I consider that the proper pronunciation. It means "dead man's river" in the Creek language.

The State Road 361 bridge crosses the Steinhatchee River and connects the towns of Steinhatchee and Jena (*Jee*-na). From the top of the bridge, you have a good view of the docks and wooden shacks that line the river's south shore and Riverside Drive. Looking down into the river is like looking into an inky abyss. It's not pollution that makes the water so black. Tannic acid naturally leaches into the river from cypress and pine trees growing along the shoreline.

Fishing, both sport and commercial, and boating are Steinhatchee's

Steinhatchee River from SR 361 Bridge

50

primary industries. Fishing in the river is a popular pastime. So is fishing or scalloping on the grass flats at the mouth of the river, called Deadman's Bay, and out in the Gulf. Two miles upriver, up State Road 51, is the Steinhatchee Landing Resort, a nature-conscious village with Old Florida–style homes and live oak– and magnolia-shaded lanes. The thirty-five-acre property wraps around a bend on the north bank of the Steinhatchee River.

I spent a weekend at Steinhatchee Landing in a two-story, tin-roofed house on a shady lane. All the houses on this lane are named for spices. Mine was the Vanilla, but it was anything but plain. It was decorated in a quaint, country-farmhouse style and furnished with comfortable, overstuffed chairs and couches. It had upstairs and downstairs screened porches with wicker rocking chairs. This is the best of both worlds: Old Florida, Cracker-style architecture built brand new with all the modern conveniences. There are thirty rental units. Most are privately owned and all are rented through the Steinhatchee Landing office. Nine of the units allow small dogs.

Developers Dean and Loretta Fowler, originally from Georgia, began building this complex in 1990. Dean first came down to Taylor County, Florida, in the late 1980s for a weekend fishing expedition at the invitation of a group of banker friends. In his gentle Georgia accent, Dean told me, "I fell in love with the Steinhatchee River and this rustic fishing village town and decided to build a vacation home here. Before long, Loretta and I were spending the majority of our spare time here. It occurred to me that it was mostly Georgia men that would come here to fish. They rarely brought their families because there wasn't much for families to do. I started thinking about what families would enjoy doing here. Then I started a scratch-pad list that evolved into the idea of a resort complex with the right amenities to attract families."

Dean had built nursing homes and retirement developments in Georgia, so he knew what a project like this entailed. He continued, "Condominium cracker boxes just wouldn't look right in this rustic little town, so I called the University of Florida School of Architecture to see if they had an expert in vintage Florida architecture. They introduced me to professor Ron Haase who had written a book called *Classic Cracker: Florida's Wood-Frame Vernacular Architecture*. Ron came up with the design criteria. He designed the first nine houses and the restaurant. Other architects have designed houses that are built here, but they follow the guidelines laid out by Ron."

The Fowlers have built a dock on the river that incorporates a renovated, sixty-year-old wooden bait store and boathouse that was half-collapsed and falling into the water when they bought the property. They have also built a horse stable, a swimming pool and spa, a children's playground, a farm animal petting zoo, jogging trails, and tennis courts. They have canoes for exploring the river and will make arrangements for guided fishing and tours. Former President Jimmy Carter, a friend of Dean and Loretta's, once brought his entire family—children and grandchildren—here for their Christmas family gathering. Reportedly, Mrs. Carter out-fished Jimmy.

When Dean first began to clear the Steinhatchee Landing property, he came across something unexpected. "I found some interesting artifacts, most of them in that small creek that runs through the property,"

Old boathouse on Steinhatchee River

Dean told me while pointing out one of the office windows. He picked up a smoky glass bottle and handed it to me. Its imperfect shape and the bubbles in the glass revealed that the bottle was old. "I found a lot of bottles, most broken but some intact like this one, probably a wine bottle. A bottle expert told me that this one dates back to the eighteen forties." I very carefully handed it back to Dean.

He continued, "Here's something else that I found in the creek." From behind the receptionist's desk, he lifted a wooden stake with a forged iron clasp around one end. "We think this might have been a tent pole. The creek yielded quite a bit of old, square-cut lumber in addition to the bottle pieces. Also, we found a still-intact and upright railing for tying horses up to. I've left it where I found it. Weeds have grown up around it, so it's hidden."

General Zachary Taylor ordered the building of Fort Frank Brooke in 1838 during the height of the Second Seminole War. There is convincing historical evidence that it was built very near or, possibly, right on the location of Steinhatchee Landing. In a *Gulf Coast Historical Review* article, historian Niles Schuh points out that reports and letters from army personnel who operated in this area during the Second Seminole War record that ". . . the falls of Steinhatchee River are six miles above Fort Frank Brooke." If their mileage estimates were accurate, this description would place the fort at the same bend in the river where Steinhatchee Landing is now. From the bottom of the river at the bend, scuba divers frequently bring up artifacts like utensils and buttons from military jackets. Maps from that time, although not detailed, show the fort at a bend in the river in approximately the same location.

Lifelong friends of mine, Michael and Leslie Poole, along with their two sons, Blake and Preston, have been making an annual weekend fishing trip to Steinhatchee for many years. It was Michael and Leslie who first told me about Steinhatchee and Steinhatchee Landing. My weekend visit overlapped with one of their annual visits, and they invited me to join them on their boat for a fishing expedition. Michael took us upriver and out onto the Gulf grass flats, where we caught trout, sea bass, and one menacing-looking, fanged thing, which Preston called a lizard fish.

The Steinhatchee Falls, referred to in those Second Seminole War records, can be reached by continuing northeast up State Road 51 about six miles to a dirt road on the right. Follow the dirt road for about a mile to the Steinhatchee River. The falls is really just an elevation change that speeds up the current over some rocks and creates a set of rapids, a rare sight in Florida. The river narrows here. Hundreds of years ago, this was the only spot where Timucuan Indians, and later Seminoles, could traverse the river on foot.

DIRECTIONS: From Highway 19, take SR 358 southwest to Jena and SR 361 north across the Steinhatchee River.

DON'T MISS: Steinhatchee Landing Resort
ADDRESSES AND EVENTS: see page 194

HIGH SPRINGS

Population: 3,863

THE SANTA FE RIVER RUNS RIGHT BY HIGH SPRINGS. Poe Springs, Blue Springs, and Ginnie Springs are just a few miles east of High Springs off County Road 340. O'Leno State Park is just north of town on Highway 441. Ichetucknee Springs State Park is only fifteen miles northeast on Highway 27. The town of High Springs can rightly claim to be at the center of north central Florida's best springs and rivers. For canoeists, kayakers, tubers, scuba divers, and cave divers, it's the ideal bivouac. It can also be an interesting place to visit for non-aquatic types as well. Downtown High Springs' selection of unique shops draws day and weekend visitors from around the state.

In 1884, the Savannah, Florida, and Western Railroad extended its tracks from Live Oak south to Gainesville. They passed through a little community known as Santaffey, named after the nearby Santa Fe River. The railroad put up a depot and a post office. Five years later, the towns-people changed the name to High Springs. (Apparently, there was once a spring on top of a hill in the middle of town.) The phosphate boom of the 1890s increased traffic, and a new rail, connecting High Springs with Tampa, opened in 1893. Two dozen trains were passing through each day. In 1896, the Plant System Railroad Line, which later merged with the Atlantic Coast Line, built a roundhouse where railroad cars could be pulled off the tracks. The railroad also built a steam engine repair and maintenance shop, a boilermaker shop, a carpentry shop, and an ice house for icing down produce in the freight cars. The town's population swelled to more than three thousand. High Springs had become a major railroad repair depot. (The original depot has been restored and now contains various business offices, but for a while it was home to a railroad museum.)

After World War II, railroad lines began converting from steam-driven engines to diesel, and High Springs' railroad business evaporated. Three decades later, the town was rediscovered as a recreational hub because of its surrounding springs and rivers. In the mid-1980s, a downtown revitalization began with the restoration of the brick, two-story, Old Opera House building (originally built in 1895) on Main Street. Its downstairs currently houses the Great Outdoors Trading Company store and café next-door to the old barbershop building built in 1915. Holding true to the Old Opera House's original purpose, the Theatre of Memory occupies the upstairs and hosts a variety of entertainers on weekend evenings.

High Springs has attracted antiques shoppers for decades. Burch Antiques, next-door to the old-fashioned Sheffield's Hardware, is a favorite. Check out the antique, English, stained-glass windows. Wisteria Cottage, Heartstrings, and High Springs Antiques Center are three others worth a visit. Two excellent bed-and-breakfasts can be found here

Burch Antiques Too

also. The Grady House is two blocks off Main Street on First Avenue, and The Rustic Inn is two miles south of town on State Road 41/27 (Main Street).

High Springs' residents have done a model job of resurrecting their town. It is an interesting place to visit, whether you're a river rat or an antiques hound. Furthermore, it has been that way for more than a decade now, which says plenty about the enthusiasm and commitment of the people who live here.

DIRECTIONS: Take I-75 to the High Springs/Highway 441 exit (Exit 399). Go west on Highway 441.

DON'T MISS: Great Outdoors Trading Company
ADDRESSES AND EVENTS: see page 195

CROSS CREEK, EVINSTON, MICANOPY, AND MCINTOSH

Population: Cross Creek 50 (estimated); Evinston 50 (estimated); Micanopy 653; McIntosh 453

THE YEARLING AND THE SECRET RIVER WERE FAVORITES OF MINE in elementary school, but I'll admit that, as an eleven-year-old, I did not fully appreciate the brilliance of premier Florida author and Pulitzer Prize winner Marjorie Kinnan Rawlings. Years later I read *Cross Creek* and, from the first page, became so engrossed in Marjorie Rawlings' world that I did little else other than eat, sleep, and read for the next day and a half until I finished it. She is funny, courageous, insightful, and almost supernatural in her understanding of both human nature and Mother Nature. She came to **Cross Creek** in 1928 to write gothic romance novels in seclusion. Instead, she found poignant drama in her own backyard. If you read *Cross Creek*, you will be compelled to go see the community that inspired it. It is a vivid picture of rural north central Florida in the 1930s. Rawlings used her typewriter as richly and colorfully as Van Gogh used his paintbrush.

    Cross Creek was fresh in my mind the first time I visited the Marjorie Kinnan Rawlings State Historic Site, and I marveled at how closely, in real life, her home matched the one in my imagination. Even the floor plan had a haunting sense of familiarity to me. I felt as if I had visited this place in a dream and knew what to expect from room to room. Here is the front porch, where Marjorie sat countless hours before her typewriter and mixed the personalities she had come to know with the stories that she wove. *Jacob's Ladder, When the Whippoorwill—, Golden Apples, Cross Creek, The Sojourner* and *The Yearling* all came to life in this very space. There is the birdbath in front of the house where, in the

Cross Creek, looking east toward Lochloosa Lake

summer, redbirds would scold her for not replenishing it with fresh, cool water. Here is the screen door that her pet raccoon, Racket, learned to open and close for himself. Here is the indoor bathroom, added five years after she moved in, between the previously separate south side and north side of the house, whose sloping floor "has proved no friend to the aged, the absent-minded and the inebriated," wrote Marjorie.

Cross Creek is less a town and more simply a place—and perhaps a state of mind. "The creek," as the locals refer to it, is an actual creek that connects Lochloosa Lake on the east side and Orange Lake on the west side. As Marjorie put it in *Cross Creek*: "Cross Creek is a bend in a country road, by land, and the flowing of Lochloosa Lake into Orange Lake, by water. We are four miles west of the small village of Island Grove, nine miles east of a turpentine still, and on the other sides we do not count distance at all, for the two lakes and the broad marshes create an infinite space between us and the horizon."

From the parking area, Rawlings' house is hidden from view by her orange grove, and the Marjorie Kinnan Rawlings State Historic Site looks like any other state park facility. But things changed when I walked through the rusty, old gate. I had a sudden, eerie sense, as if I had stepped back seventy years in time. As I followed a dirt path through the orange trees (it is still a producing grove), I could smell the sweet citrus. Between the rows of trees, pine logs were stacked, ready to light in the event of a freeze, as Marjorie described in her chapter on winter. Back then, the sounding of the train whistle at midnight was everyone's warning when the temperature dropped to freezing. Grove hands and neighbors alike would spend all night lighting and stoking fires throughout the grove in a desperate attempt to keep the crop warm enough to make it through the chill. On the left side of the grove is a chicken coop (with chickens in it), and on the right side is the barn, filled with old farming implements. Just beyond the barn is the house. Seeing it, I was again haunted by the distinct feeling that I had arrived at a place where I had lived in a previous life. It wasn't déjà vu—just that her descriptions were so indelibly imprinted in my mind: "It sat snugly then as now under tall old orange trees, and had a simple grace of line, low, rambling and one-storied."

It was Marjorie Rawlings' wish that, after her passing, her house be kept as it was when she lived there, and the curators have done a marvelous job of honoring that request. She left it to the University of Florida Foundation, which maintained it from her death in 1953 until donating it to the Florida Department of Natural Resources in 1970. Historians think the house was built around 1890. It is a true Florida Cracker structure with white board-and-batten sides and a lichen-covered, cedar-shingle roof. There's a duck pen to one side and a simple vegetable garden and an outhouse out back. Inside, down a short hallway leading from the south porch, I spotted a tomcat sleeping in a wicker basket and wondered if he was a descendent of Marjorie's cat, Jib.

Jars of fruit and jam sit on the kitchen windowsill. By all appearances, someone still lives here. The well-worn floors are painted ochre green, and the paneled walls have a fresh coat of white. The house is made up of, more or less, three sections. The back (southwest) section contains the kitchen and dining room. Here, Marjorie prepared and served alligator, pounded, floured, and quick-fried in butter; deep-fried soft-shell cooter (turtle); and blackbird pie. She also made egg croquettes, cooked Crab Newburg, and baked an assortment of cakes and pies for desserts. She delighted in good food and cooking and wrote

Marjorie Kinnan Rawlings' house at Cross Creek

about it in great detail in *Cross Creek Cookery*, as well as in the "Our Daily Bread" chapter of *Cross Creek*: "Cookery is my one vanity and I am a slave to any guest who praises my culinary art."

The north section of the house contains two bedrooms and the previously mentioned indoor bathroom. In the living room in the front (southeast) section, there is a photograph of Marjorie on the fireplace mantle. In it, she holds a shotgun comfortably under one arm, while her pointer, Pat, sits attentively at her feet. The most magical part of the house is the front porch, where she did all of her writing. You can almost hear her old typewriter clacking.

Valerie Rivers has been the site manager at the Marjorie Kinnan Rawlings State Historic Site for many years. She told me, "This site, because it recreates so well what she wrote about, is an exciting—or a better word is—fulfilling experience for anyone who has read her." When I told her how enthralled I was with Marjorie's writing and her depiction of Cross Creek, Valerie suggested I might enjoy reading *The Creek* by J. T. "Jake" Glisson, which offers a different perspective on Cross Creek. "He grew up just down the road from here during the time when Marjorie Rawlings was doing most of her writing," she told me.

Marjorie referred to the Glisson family numerous times in *Cross Creek*, and J. T. was a young boy who became her good friend. I made a mental note to look for *The Creek*.

"Have you been in to Evinston yet?" Valerie asked. She pronounced it "Ivinston" with a short *i*. Before leaving to visit Evinston, I followed directions Valerie had given me to Antioch Cemetery, where Marjorie Rawlings is buried—out County Road 325 to Island Grove and across Highway 301 on SE 219 Avenue. From there it's two miles to SE 225 Drive, a well-graded dirt road, and another two miles to the right fork at SE 189 Avenue. Valerie had told me to walk through the gate, toward the center of the cemetery, and look for an azalea bush. It was right where she said it would be.

Marjorie Rawlings died quite suddenly of a brain hemorrhage in 1953. She was only fifty-seven years old. Norton Baskin, Marjorie's second husband, had said that she had wanted to be buried at a small cemetery in Citra, just south of Island Grove. Apparently through some miscommunication between Norton and the funeral home, she was inadvertently buried in the wrong cemetery.

Rawlings' grave is a simple, flat, marble slab with no headstone. No signs lead you to it. No fence surrounds it. Nothing distinguishes it from anyone else's grave. Her epitaph reads, "Marjorie Kinnan Rawlings, 1896–1953, Wife of Norton Baskin, Through her writing she endeared herself to the people of the world." On my most recent visit there, I found a new marble slab next to Marjorie's: "Norton Baskin, 1901–1997, Beloved Husband."

Evinston is a tiny community across Orange Lake, on the north side of Cross Creek. I followed Valerie's directions back north on County Road 325 and stopped on the bridge that crosses the creek. Although they had no formal local government, the inhabitants of Cross Creek would meet here regularly to settle matters that concerned the community. It was also the Saturday night socializing spot. It was a serene setting and appeared little changed from seventy years before. The water was black, and dead leaves looked like glitter floating on the surface. The creek flows imperceptibly from Lochloosa Lake, past a floating dock attached to a cypress tree, under the bridge, and out into wide-open Orange Lake.

I continued down County Road 325 to County Road 346 and turned left. Orange Lake appeared again on my left, so I pulled off the road beside a pasture to take in the view. When I turned off my car's motor, I heard a clucking, cooing sound coming from just over a rise. Suddenly, a dozen sandhill cranes rose and sailed across the road. When I walked up the crest of the rise, I saw what all the commotion was about. A convention of what must have been at least three hundred sandhill cranes (and a few resident cows) was in session. Devout birdwatchers consider this area (along with nearby Payne's Prairie) prime for spotting these tall, gray, migratory, grazing birds. They arrive annually in late fall and spend most of their time here eating the small grains that are planted in winter for the cattle. They stay until March, when all at once they take to the air and, for several days, circle overhead in huge flocks. Then, just as suddenly, they leave.

County Road 225 makes a sharp, right-to-left S-turn that signals your arrival at Evinston. On the right is the old Wood's Packinghouse, erected in the early 1900s, and just beyond is the Wood & Swink Store and Post Office, a wood-frame structure with a tin roof. Micanopy merchant S. H. Benjamin built the store in 1882 as a warehouse to store freight offloaded from the railroad. Two years later, the local postmaster purchased it and used it intermittently as a store and post office. In 1913, it became the permanent post office and today appears on the National Register of Historic Places. Fred Wood Jr.'s book, *Evinston Home: God's Country*, was my source for some interesting local history.

In 1905, H. D. Wood and his brother-in-law, R. C. Evins, acquired the store following the hasty exit of the previous owner, John Hester. Apparently, while standing in the front door of his store, Hester shot and killed Watt Barron and wounded his father, J. F. Barron. One version of the story claims that the shooting resulted from an argument over who had the best-looking field of watermelons. Regardless of the cause, Hester was out and the Wood family was in. (In-law Paul Swink was a partner for just a couple years in the 1930s, and his name was left on the sign.) The Evinston store and post office remains in the Wood family today. Wilma Sue Wood, Fred Wood Jr.'s wife, has been the postmaster and store manager since 1979.

From the outside, it looks exactly like what it is: a 120-some-odd-year-

Counter in Wood and Swink Store and Post Office, Evinston

old country general store. Just inside the door on the left, a partition wall with a post office service window in the middle stands, surrounded by old-style post office boxes. Sixteen of them date back to 1882. There is a single "Wanted" poster on the bulletin board beneath the service window. An ancient cash register, a dozen jars of various home-pickled vegetables, and a row of fishbowl-shaped cookie jars sit atop a glass candy counter on the left, past the post office boxes. Tea, spices, cigars, and other general store sundries sit on the shelves behind the counter. On the top shelf, several wooden boxes with "Winchester Small Arms Ammunition" stamped on the side look as though they have collected a few decades of dust. A big, old, wood-burning stove sits in the center of the store, surrounded by rocking chairs. If only that stove could speak.

The first time I visited the Wood & Swink Store, Wilma Wood introduced me to Jake Glisson's wife, Pat, who happened to be in the store while I was buying a copy of Jake's *The Creek*. Pat and J. T. "Jake" Glisson have lived in Evinston since the early 1960s. They raised their five children here. Of course, Jake grew up across Orange Lake in Cross Creek.

I asked Pat to tell me a little about her and Jake, and she offered, "Jake's at home right now. He was just raking leaves in the front yard when I left. Why don't you come on over to the house and meet him?"

I followed Pat Glisson to a beautiful, turn-of-the-century house. Jake and a large but friendly Doberman greeted us at the door. After introductions and some explanation about what I was researching, Jake offered me a seat and some of Pat's low-cal Christmas cookies. I asked him to tell me about *The Creek*.

"If you should discover that there were never any fences in Hannibal, Missouri," Jake began with a chuckle, "don't try to tell anyone, 'cause they'll hate you for it." He was referring to a talk that he gave before a historical society. He thought that they, of all people, would appreciate hearing about a viewpoint on Cross Creek different from Rawlings'. "I had launched into it," he explained, "and the ones that weren't going to sleep were getting hostile. About halfway through, I just switched in midstream and went to some little anecdotes. It was either a case of leaving town tarred and feathered, or just going with it their way!"

Jake grew up almost next door to Marjorie Rawlings. They became close friends, even though his dad and Marjorie did not always see eye to eye. In *The Creek*, which I have since read, Jake tells marvelous stories that illustrate what life was like for a kid growing up in Cross Creek. He was a firsthand witness to many of the events about which Marjorie wrote, so some of his stories overlap with hers, but he tells them his way. "I thought that writers in a historical society would be interested in the license that Mrs. Rawlings used in writing, for instance, *Cross Creek*. Just that slight little deviation that can change the meaning, and in some cases was a little imaginary. I feel that it was part of her brilliance, that she did a little patchwork here and there—ever so delicately." Jake's love and respect for Marjorie Rawlings are apparent, particularly in the chapter "That Woman Next Door." His point was that sometimes writers adjust things a little to make them fit, and Marjorie was no different in that respect. Re-hearing those stories from a different viewpoint was one of the things that made his book so fascinating.

For Jake, writing *The Creek* was a return to his childhood. He told me, "The truth is, the day I finished the book I was a little depressed. Because in writing it, it was kind of like I went back there and did it all again. It was a fun experience."

Jake has been an artist much longer than he's been a writer. He is a graduate of the Ringling School of Art and Design in Sarasota. His brightly hued watercolor paintings and illustrations have appeared in magazines and books (including, of course, his own). His artwork has been displayed around the world. Most of it depicts nature in central Florida. We began talking about the sandhill cranes (one of his favorite subjects to paint), and he explained about the cranes in one of his paintings on his wall. "For the longest time I thought that this dancelike thing that they do was sort of a mating ritual. They get a leaf or a sprig of moss, and they keep it in the air—three or four of them—and this will go on for a long time. I call it the leaf dance—they just keep flippin' it up, flippin' it up with their wings. I really don't know why they do it. The older I get, the more I realize that none of us really knows an awful lot about nature. The minute you say, 'This is the reason why,' it will make a fool of you."

Before I left, I asked Jake if he thought Evinston still looked the same as it did when he was a boy. He surprised me when he said that he had never been to Evinston until he and Pat moved here thirty years ago. When they decided to move back to this general area, Pat looked at a house in Evinston. When she tried to describe to Jake where it was— "You know, you go past the store and turn right, and it's that second house"—he had to confess, "Honey, I'm sorry, I hate to tell you, but, although I spent my whole childhood only five miles on the other side of the lake from there, I've never been to Evinston." It was all the way across Orange Lake from Cross Creek, and in those days it might as well have been across the Atlantic Ocean. The creek was its own world, and in some ways it still is.

The time I spent visiting with the Glissons will go down in my mental diary with an asterisk. Their hospitality toward a complete stranger— particularly one wielding a tape recorder—is a vestige of a kinder era. Talking to them allowed me the privilege of visiting, if only briefly, that era, and I'll be forever grateful to them for that.

I dropped by the Wood & Swink Store recently and found it unchanged from the first time I visited. Wilma told me that Jake and Pat were well and that Jake was still much in demand as a speaker for historical groups. Since I was gathering updated information for this volume, I asked her if the store's phone number had changed. "You know what?" she replied. "We don't have a phone—never really needed one."

"Charming" seems to be the word most frequently used to describe **Micanopy,** a tiny community just twelve miles south of Gainesville. The town's several-block-long main street, Cholokka Road, rolls past tin-roofed frame houses and century-old, awning-shaded, brick storefronts. Wide-spreading branches from huge live oaks form a tunnel over the road. At one time, this was Highway 441, but in the 1960s the state rebuilt the highway, and the Department of Transportation opted to bypass Micanopy. It probably seemed like a death toll then but is now considered a godsend.

Spanish explorer Hernando de Soto came across Timucuan Indians living near here in 1539, and there is archaeological evidence that suggests that this area was populated prior to the Timucuans, perhaps as far back as ten thousand years ago. In 1774, naturalist William Bartram visited the Seminole village at Cuscawilla, also very near here, while collecting botanical specimens. His book, *Travels,* is one of the earliest reliable sources of information on Florida's plant life, wildlife, geography, and Seminole Indians. An actual town was not established here until 1821. That makes it Florida's second oldest town and its oldest inland town. It was called Wanton's Trading Post then. In 1835, the name officially changed to Micanopy, in honor of Chief Micanopy, head of the Seminole nation. The naming of the town seems ironic to me. The United States government was trying to force the Seminoles to move to reservations west of the Mississippi. They revolted and, later that same year, Chief Micanopy led the attack known as the Dade Massacre, marking the beginning of the Second Seminole War.

One town icon is the Herlong Mansion. This grand, red-brick, Southern plantation house with Greek Revival characteristics is appropriately referred to as a mansion. Out front, four massive, Corinthian columns support the roof over full-width verandahs both upstairs and down. The carefully renovated turn-of-the-century interior has leaded-glass windows; twelve-foot-high ceilings; mahogany, maple, and oak floors; quarter-sawn tiger-oak paneling; and ten fireplaces.

Zetty Herlong operated a prosperous lumber business in southern

Alabama until one tragic day in 1907, when a fire destroyed both his business and his home. Herlong and his wife, Natalie, moved to Micanopy, into what was then a simple, two-story, wood-frame house that was built sometime in the 1840s (the original deed is long lost) by Natalie's parents, the Simontons. Natalie had inherited it around the turn of the century. Zetty restarted his lumber business in Micanopy and also became a prominent citrus farmer. In 1909, the Herlongs decided to remodel the old house and actually constructed the brick version that stands today around the original.

When Natalie passed away in 1950, her six siblings—four sisters and two brothers—inherited equal shares of the house, and an eighteen-year battle for sole ownership ensued. Finally, sister Inez was granted legal possession, but on the very first day of her ownership, while cleaning in the second-floor bedroom that she and her sister Mae had shared during childhood, Inez collapsed and went into a diabetic coma. She died shortly thereafter, never having gotten to see her long-sought-after house returned to its original splendor.

In 1990, Sonny Howard purchased the Herlong house from Kim and Simone Evans, who had been operating it as a weekend bed-and-breakfast since 1987. After all the paperwork was signed, the Evanses told Sonny about some unusual occurrences in the mansion.

Historic restoration specialists from Wisconsin were the first to report odd happenings. They were staying in the house overnight while restoring the floors back in 1987. Three nights in a row they heard footsteps and doors opening and closing on the second floor. No one was up there. On the fourth night, they moved into a motel. Sonny told me, "I was quick to point out to the Evanses that working with drums of paint stripper for three days straight might be more than enough to incline someone to hear ghosts." But the eerie activity didn't end there.

I asked Sonny what other kinds of things have happened. "Nothing scary. Just odd things, subtle things. Lately we've noticed perfume smells—lilac or gardenia—but only in Mae's room. We don't use any kind of fragrant cleaners. Sometimes the door to Mae's room locks or unlocks by itself. There have been some odd instances in that room with the window shade, the clock radio, even the Tootsie Rolls that we leave bedside."

Guests and visitors report the most interesting occurrences, usually

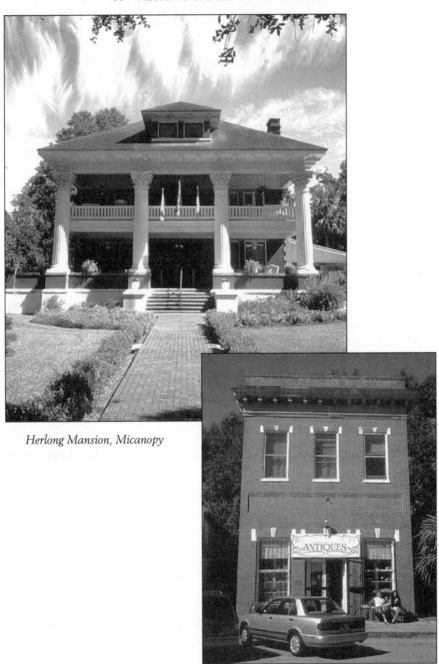

Herlong Mansion, Micanopy

*Antique shopping on Cholokka Boulevard,
Micanopy*

over breakfast the following morning. Some have had very vivid and odd dreams. One even saw the image in a mirror of a woman wearing a red shawl. Almost all the occurrences take place in Mae's room or in the hall just outside. Scientists from the Center for Paranormal Studies in Ocala have investigated here twice. Once, they found anomalous electromagnetic readings in the hallway on the second floor.

If there is a ghost, Inez seems to be the likely culprit. Some guests have even reported that she looks after them by tidying up after them, putting their things away in dresser drawers, and locking guest room doors after they turn in for the night. If it is Inez, I'm sure she's delighted. The mansion has been beautifully restored, and the interior is filled with antique furnishings. Lon and Julie Boggs bought the Herlong Mansion from Sonny in 2001 and have continued the bed-and-breakfast's tradition of gracious accommodations and great food.

Downtown Micanopy is an antiquer's and book lover's paradise. It is only three blocks long, but there are more than a dozen antiques and curio shops in those three blocks. Most of the buildings date back to the beginning of the twentieth century. Huge, ancient oak trees filled with Spanish moss shade the entire district. Shopping for old stuff—old books at O. Brisky Books (in the 1885 Benjamin Building), vintage clothing at The Twisted Sister, and antiques at a dozen shops—draws visitors to Micanopy seven days a week. Some shops have specialties. At the Micanopy Country Store antiques shop (housed in the 1903 Feaster Building), I met David Keifer, who collects old glassware including wine bottles, mason jars, and milk bottles. His oldest dates to the mid-1800s. In the next block over, at Antiques Mall Downtown, vintage postcards are the specialty. There is only one restaurant in town. Thank goodness it's a good one. The Old Florida Café serves well-stuffed sandwiches, salads, and soups. Try the King Ranch Chili.

If your interest in the old extends beyond shopping, then visit the Micanopy Historical Museum in the restored 1890 J. E. Thrasher farm implement warehouse, or visit the Micanopy Cemetery off Seminary Road (east from the center of town). A sign at the gate tells visitors that the cemetery was established in 1826. The further into the cemetery you walk, the bigger the oak trees and the older the headstones. Near the back you'll find the Herlong headstone. It is one of the larger ones, in keeping with the family's stature. The oaks here are so dense that they form a single, massive canopy of branches and Spanish moss that darkens the place, even in the middle of the afternoon. You might not want to go alone.

Between Micanopy and Ocala, Highway 441 rolls across scenic pastureland and into the quiet hamlet of **McIntosh.** Avenue G, which has the town's only traffic light (a blinking one), is a good place to start your visit. Huge live oaks grace every yard, their Spanish moss–covered limbs spreading out over the tops of homes and across streets. They must be centuries old. Some have trunks as big around as small houses (and look as though elves live inside them). I've never seen so many grand oak trees in one place. Two of the grandest are in the front yard and backyard of Margie Karow's Merrily Bed and Breakfast on the south side of Avenue G. The Merrily is a yellow, two-story folk Victorian with a steeply pitched tin roof and black shutters. W. E. Allen, McIntosh's first postmaster, built the house in 1888. Margie must have a green thumb. Ferns, flowers, and caladiums fill her entire yard.

Most of the other houses along McIntosh's avenues (B through H) are also one-hundred-plus-year-old Victorians—some restored, some not. They were originally the homes of citrus and cotton farmers whose fields surrounded the town. After the big freezes of 1894 and 1895, the farmers switched to vegetables—crookneck squash, cabbage, lettuce. I'm told that the old Gist House, at the corner of Avenue H and Fifth Street, was built with the revenues of a single season's crookneck squash crop. Another farmer grew iceberg lettuce exclusively for the ocean liner *Queen Mary* and shipped it by train to New York.

A few blocks past the Merrily, at the end of Avenue G, is McIntosh's restored railroad depot. Originally constructed in 1884 by the old Florida Southern Railroad, it was scheduled to be torn down in 1974. In 1973, a group of townsfolk who felt the depot was a valuable landmark formed the Friends of McIntosh to try to save it. It is now McIntosh's Historical Museum.

McIntosh postmaster Sharon Little is one of the original founders of the Friends of McIntosh. She moved here in 1972 and became postmaster in 1981. Sharon told me, "We formed the Friends of McIntosh in nineteen seventy-three just to save the depot. We needed to purchase it from the railroad and move it six feet back from the track. Six thousand dollars is what we had to come up with, and we decided that the best way to raise that would be to hold a little festival right here in the park. Our first Eighteen-Nineties Festival was in nineteen seventy-four. We had twenty-five vendors and drew about thirty-five hundred people." The 1890s Festival has run every year since, on either the third or fourth weekend in October (so as not to conflict with a Gator game). It now draws forty thousand people and features tours of McIntosh's historic homes, storytelling, a parade, more than three hundred vendors, and all-day live entertainment.

In the 1930s and '40s, as the more fertile land in south Florida began to be cultivated, farming around McIntosh faded. Today it is primarily a bedroom community for people who work in Ocala (seventeen miles south) and in Gainesville (seventeen miles north). Without any new industry moving in after the 1940s, McIntosh never experienced a surge in new housing. At the time, things may have seemed bleak, but the long-term blessing in disguise is that most of the turn-of-the-century Victorian houses were not torn down, leaving McIntosh the tranquil and historic village it is today.

DIRECTIONS: Take I-75 to the Micanopy exit (Exit 374). Go west two miles to Cholokka Road. Go south one mile to Micanopy. From Micanopy to Evinston (5 miles), take Highway 441 south to CR 346, go east to CR 225, and go south. From Micanopy to Cross Creek/Marjorie Kinnan Rawlings State Historic Site (14 miles), take Highway 441 south to CR 346, go east to CR 325, and go south. Or from Highway 301, turn northeast on CR 325 at Island Grove to Cross Creek. To reach McIntosh, take Highway 441 south from Micanopy, or take Exit 368 off I-75, follow SR 318 east to Highway 441, and go north.

DON'T MISS: The Marjorie Kinnan Rawlings State Historic Site in Cross Creek; the Wood & Swink Store and Post Office in Evinston; the Herlong Mansion in Micanopy; and the Railroad Depot Historical Museum in McIntosh
ADDRESSES AND EVENTS: see page 195–196

CRESCENT CITY
AND WELAKA

Population: Crescent City 1,776; Welaka 586

US ROUTE 17 NORTH OUT OF DELAND IS A SCENIC, ALBEIT LEISURELY, alternative to the concrete monotony of Interstate 95. This is fern-growing country, and the mesh tarp–covered fields are plentiful along the way. Before long, US 17 brings you to **Crescent City,** which rests atop a bluff on the curved (hence "crescent") west bank of Crescent Lake.

The first families settled here in 1852, and a few more came in the late 1860s. In 1875, Charles Griffing bought most of the property and divided it into single-acre home lots and five-acre citrus groves. Griffing's wife, Jennie, changed the name of what was then Dunn's Lake to Crescent Lake because its shape reminded her of the crescent moon. The new town adopted the name of the lake.

US Route 17 becomes Summit Street when it passes through downtown Crescent City. Turn east onto Central Avenue and follow it four blocks downhill to Crescent Lake and you'll find docks with covered boathouses lining the shore. This lake, like many others, once claimed to be "the bass capital of the world." However, Crescent City's big annual event is the Catfish Festival, held the first weekend in April. The agenda includes bluegrass music, arts and crafts displays, and a parade, but the highlight is the catfish skinning contest.

There are some interesting turn-of-the-century houses here and along the waterfront. One is the charming Victorian Sprague House, a couple of blocks up from the lake at 125 Central Avenue. Built in 1892, it was originally an inn run by Kate Sprague. In recent years, it has been a restaurant and a bed-and-breakfast. Unfortunately, as of this writing, it is closed. Another is the Hubbard House, a private residence at 600 North Park Street. It's a Queen Anne Victorian built by botanist Henry Hubbard in 1879.

Back at the top of the hill, at the intersection of Central Avenue and Summit Street, Total Interiors, an antiques, collectibles, and home decor shop, occupies the restored, two-story brick People's Bank building. On the Central Avenue side of the corner, this building connects with a quaint, tin-roofed, wood-frame house with a white picket fence and a big mulberry tree in the front yard.

Continue north on Highway 17, then veer west on Putnam County Road 308B to **Welaka,** the real "bass capital." Welaka, a variation of the Seminole Indian name for the St. Johns River, *Ylacco,* sits on a bluff overlooking the St. Johns at one of its most scenic points. Michael and Leslie Poole, my Florida fishing-getaway experts (they also put me onto Steinhatchee) told me about it. Bass-fishing enthusiasts rent boats or bring their own and stay at rustic fishing lodges and cabins on the river, like Bass Haven Lodge, Andersen's Lodge, and the less rustic Floridian Sports Club. There's good fresh seafood at these places too. I had excellent fried grouper fingers at Lure's Restaurant, an old tongue-and-groove wooden cabin overlooking the river at Andersen's Lodge. Fishing lures hang on the walls and from wagon wheels attached to the ceiling at Lure's.

DIRECTIONS: North of DeLand on US 17 to Crescent City. Continue north on US 17 to CR 308B, then turn west to CR 309 and Welaka.

DON'T MISS: The view of the St. Johns River from Lure's Restaurant in Welaka
ADDRESSES AND EVENTS: see page 197

CEDAR KEY

Population: 790

YOU HAVE TO SEE IT ON A MAP TO FULLY APPRECIATE how far out into the Gulf the town of Cedar Key sits. The drive west on Highway 24 from Otter Creek (at Highway 19) to the cluster of islands called the Cedar Keys is long, straight, and uninterrupted. Downtown Cedar Key and Dock Street, its floating restaurant-and-gift-shop extension, are actually on Way Key. This is probably what Key West looked like forty years ago.

Most of the houses at the northwest end of Second Street, downtown's main street, have been or are being restored. Quite a few were built in the 1870s and 1880s, when the town was experiencing its cedar lumber industry boom. Lumber mills on adjacent keys milled cedar for making pencils. A. W. Faber had a mill on Atsena Otie Key, half a mile offshore from Way Key. Fishing and shipping were also important in Cedar Key. Florida's first cross-state railroad, the Atlantic to Gulf/Florida Railroad Company Line, completed in 1861, ran from Fernandina to Cedar Key.

Cedar Key has a history of attracting famous writers and visionaries. John D. MacDonald wrote many of his Travis McGee books here, and he sometimes used Cedar Key as a setting for his novels. John Muir concluded his one-thousand-mile walk from Indiana to the Gulf of Mexico in Cedar Key in October 1867. He remained here for several months to study the eco-structure of the coast. From Cedar Key, he moved to California, where, two years later, he helped establish Yosemite National Park and the Sierra Club.

Cedar Key's most famous landmark, The Island Hotel, has survived ravaging hurricanes, floods, fires, and the Civil War. It was built in 1859

Fishing from Dock Street Pier

with an oak-beam frame and one-foot-thick oyster-shell tabby walls. Located on Second Street between A and B Streets, it still appears identical to turn-of-the-century photos of it. It was originally built as Parsons and Hale's General Store. When Union troops invaded the town, they burned most of the buildings but left the store standing because they needed it to house supplies and troops. No doubt this was a frustrating time for the owner, Maj. John Parsons, who commanded a detachment of Confederate volunteers.

Following the war, Parsons and his partner, Francis Hale, reopened the general store, which John Muir described in his journal. "I stepped into a little store, which had a considerable trade in quinine, and alligator and rattlesnake skins. . . ." Sometime in the 1880s, Parsons and Hale began taking boarders and serving meals. In 1896, before hurricanes were assigned names, a furious hurricane hit Cedar Key, devastating most of the town but leaving the store intact. Most people mark the 1896 hurricane as the end of Cedar Key's prosperous industrial period.

In 1915, Simon Feinberg, a property investor, bought the building and remodeled it into the Bay Hotel. In the years that followed, the hotel changed names and owners frequently. During the Depression, one owner tried to burn it down, but the fire department was just across the street, and firemen saved it.

Everyone seems to agree that the hotel's heyday began in 1946, when Bessie and Loyal Gibbs bought it and renamed it the Island Hotel. Previous owners had operated a brothel out of the place during the decade or so before, and it had become quite rundown. Bessie and Loyal toiled exhaustedly to put the hotel back into shape. Gibby ran the bar and Bessie ran the restaurant. In 1948, they hired artist Helen Tooker to paint the picture of King Neptune that still hangs behind the bar today. That painting, like the hotel, seems to be blessed with multiple lives. It has survived gunshots, hurricanes, and even flooding, when a 1950 hurricane tore part of the hotel's roof off. Bessie's culinary skills, restaurant-operating talent, and panache with the clientele won the couple fame and customers. Loyal died in 1962, and Bessie, while still operating the hotel, went on to become Cedar Key's mayor from 1967 to 1968. She also started the very popular Annual Arts and Crafts Festival, and she was instrumental in getting the Cedar Key Museum open. With her health deteriorating, she sold the Island Hotel in 1974 and died the following year.

Over the decades, the Island Hotel has been host to Florida politicians; famous writers like Pearl Buck and John D. McDonald; actresses and actors; and singers like Tennessee Ernie Ford and, more recently, Jimmy Buffet, who would sometimes perform impromptu in the Neptune Bar during the 1970s.

Like the island of Cedar Key, the Island Hotel is rustic, with well-weathered wood and some cracked plaster on its exterior, although current owners Dawn and Tony Cousins have been doing a fine job of restoring the place piece by piece. The restaurant is still famous for its native Florida seafood dishes like soft-shell blue crab, and for its hearts-of-palm salad, Bessie's recipe.

Two blocks west of downtown, Dock Street swings out over the water. Gift shops, eateries, and a few galleries occupy the wood buildings. The eateries include several seafood restaurants, all with similar menu items—fresh grouper, shrimp, lobster, oysters, and clams. I like Pat's Red Luck Café, named after a local pirate legend. Owner Pat

Hibbitz moved his restaurant from the other end of Dock Street to its current location in 2002. The upstairs view from the screened porch, overlooking the Gulf, Atsena Otie Key, and the coastline north, is unbeatable. My favorite is the Captain's Platter with fish, shrimp, and oysters (offered fried or grilled). The Dock Street galleries feature island-theme paintings, sculpture, pottery, and wall-hangings. Stop in at The Suwannee Triangle Gallery to see some beautiful watercolors. Others are The Water's Edge and Island Gallery (an old favorite of mine, The Wild Women Gallery, has relocated in one end), and The Sawgrass Gallery. Upstairs, the Sawgrass rents out two quaint and colorful motel rooms.

There are more shops and galleries on Second Street. The Cedar Keyhole has a great collection of Ron Dahline pottery face jugs, and the Pen Names Bookstore keeps a thorough inventory of Florida-related books. The most fascinating shop in Cedar Key has to be The Natural Experience, at the south end of Second Street, where owner Don Duden lathe-turns and carves pieces of driftwood into beautiful sculpture. You can watch Don work in his carving shop, which is glassed in at the back corner of the gallery.

Not too many towns this size can boast two historical museums. The Cedar Key Historical Society operates a museum downtown at the corner of State Road 24 and Second Street. The Cedar Key State Museum is off Way Key and a little more difficult to find. Just follow the signs, which are everywhere in town.

Two annual festivals bring visitors from around the state. The Seafood Festival, celebrated every year since 1969, is the third weekend in October. The Sidewalk Arts Festival is held the second or third weekend in April.

DIRECTIONS: From Highway 19 at Otter Creek, take SR 24 southwest.

DON'T MISS: The Island Hotel
ADDRESSES AND EVENTS: see page 197-198

CENTRAL REGION

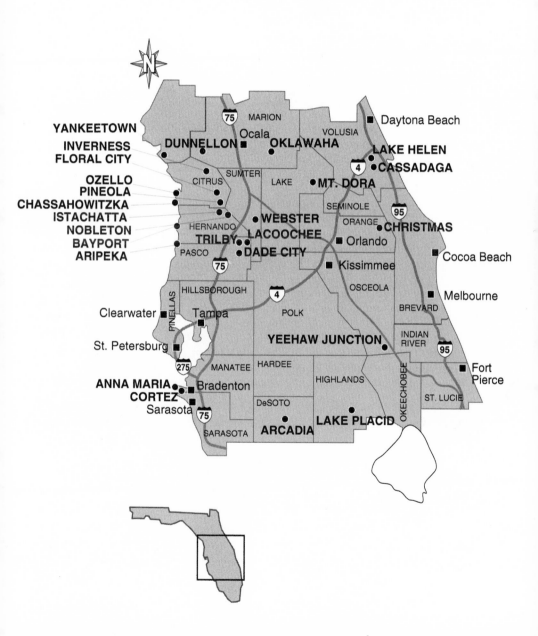

YANKEETOWN
INVERNESS
FLORAL CITY

OZELLO
PINEOLA
CHASSAHOWITZKA
ISTACHATTA
NOBLETON
BAYPORT
ARIPEKA

DUNNELLON

MARION
Ocala
OKLAWAHA

Daytona Beach

VOLUSIA

LAKE HELEN
CASSADAGA

SUMTER
CITRUS

LAKE

MT. DORA

SEMINOLE

ORANGE

CHRISTMAS

WEBSTER
LACOOCHEE
TRILBY
HERNANDO
DADE CITY
PASCO

Orlando

Cocoa Beach

Kissimmee

OSCEOLA

Melbourne

Clearwater
Tampa

HILLSBOROUGH

POLK

BREVARD

St. Petersburg

YEEHAW JUNCTION

INDIAN
RIVER

ANNA MARIA
CORTEZ
Sarasota

MANATEE

HARDEE

Bradenton

HIGHLANDS

DeSOTO

LAKE PLACID

ARCADIA

SARASOTA

Fort
Pierce

ST. LUCIE

OKEECHOBEE

YANKEETOWN

Population: 629

FLORIDA'S BIG BEND AREA—NOW OFFICIALLY CALLED THE NATURE COAST and sometimes unofficially referred to as the Cracker Coast—starts somewhere north of New Port Richey and curves around to somewhere east of Lighthouse Point, south of Tallahassee. What distinguishes it from the rest of Florida's coast is that there are essentially no beaches here. The sea bottom, extending for miles out into the Gulf of Mexico, is seldom deeper than six feet. Because of this shallow shelf, there is very little wave action to build up a beach. Without beaches, there are no high-rise condos, no hotels, no T-shirt shops, no throngs of Bermuda shorts–clad tourists. The Big Bend coastline is mostly grass flats and marsh. Some of Florida's most scenic, spring-fed rivers empty into the Gulf in this stretch, and some lightly populated fishing villages have grown up around these areas. Yankeetown is one of these. It sits on the Withlacoochee River a few miles inland from the Gulf down Levy County Road 40, west of Highway 19.

This is a town that experienced brief national fame twice during the 1960s. First, during the 1960 Nixon-Kennedy presidential campaigns, the townsfolk held a debate and a straw election. The news wires picked up the story, and it was a national topic for several days. Nixon won in Yankeetown.

Yankeetown's second brush with fame came in the summer of 1961, when the Mirisch Company and United Artists came here to make a movie based on Richard Powell's novel *Pioneer, Go Home*. For the big screen, the title was changed to *Follow That Dream*. It starred Elvis Presley, who stayed in Yankeetown for two months. Elvis fans came from far and wide to see their idol making his ninth major motion picture. Extra traffic police had to be brought in to keep the crowds at bay. One of the main film set locations was a bridge where County Road 40 crosses Bird Creek about a mile from where it dead-ends into the Gulf. Locals have renamed County Road 40 from Highway 19 west the Follow That Dream Parkway.

See Yankeetown! signs, made from a single horizontal board with one end sawed to a point, could be found alongside many of north Florida's and Georgia's rutted roads in the 1920s and 1930s, long before *See Rock City!* became a common sight. They advertised a riverside retreat at Honey Bluff along the Withlacoochee River. The original name for the retreat was going to be Knotts, named after A. F. Knotts, a U. S. Steel Corporation attorney, former Indiana state representative, and former mayor of Hammond, Indiana. After his retirement, Knotts came to Florida in search of a place to build a camp for fishing and hunting. He wanted it to be on a freshwater, navigable stream.

Knotts had handled all the land transactions when U. S. Steel built the town of Gary, Indiana, in 1905, so he was quite familiar with founding communities. Initially, he purchased some property on Crystal River but in 1920 found that he liked the Honey Bluff area on the Withlacoochee River better. He advertised the location to his friends back in Indiana. Some came and built shanties with Knotts alongside the river. To get there, they had to travel by rail to Dunnellon, then ride twenty-five miles to the coast with Hugh Coleman, the Star route mail carrier. It was Coleman who started calling the place Yankeetown, since he was carrying so many Yankees to Knotts' fishing camp. The name stuck. A. F.'s nephew, Eugene Knotts, suggested that he build a lodge on the river to be run by Eugene and his wife, Norma, to accommodate shorter term visitors. Completed in 1924, this would become the Izaak Walton Lodge, named after seventeenth-century English author Sir Izaak Walton, who was best known for *The Compleat Angler,* his treatise on the art and virtues of fishing and in praise of a simpler and more leisurely lifestyle.

Today, Yankeetown still holds true to its original premise. It meanders, like a snake, alongside the Withlacoochee for about six miles. Wayne and Linda Harrington purchased the Izaak Walton Lodge in 1987 and restored it to perfection. They also opened a restaurant in the lodge, called The Compleat Angler, with Linda's brother, gourmet chef James Brauer, at the helm.

But on July 22, 1999, disaster struck when the wooden lodge caught fire. Except for the kitchen, most of the building was destroyed. The Harringtons, ever determined, rebuilt and reopened fourteen months later. The new lodge, while not an exact replica, pays fine homage to the original. Moss-filled oaks shade the rustic restaurant and lodge, which overlooks a bend in the Withlacoochee River at the end of Sixty-third Street. The Withlacoochee winds three and a half miles down to the Gulf from here. Otters, manatees, and alligators are common sights along the river, and sometimes even dolphins are spotted swimming up this far.

The Compleat Angler Restaurant retains its excellent menu, with wonderful seafood dishes as well as some exotic fare, like the Wild Game Platter with Blackened Venison and Smoked Grilled Boar in Rosemary Sauce. Sauces are one of Chef Brauer's specialties. The first time I dined at the Compleat Angler, I had the Mustard Shrimp Appetizer, with its creamy mustard-and-scallions sauce. For my entrée, I had the Broiled Snapper Monte Carlo, topped with lump blue crab, asparagus, and hollandaise. Both were delectable and are still favorites on the menu.

After that dinner, I drove the extra few miles down County Road 40 to its terminus at the Gulf. Land gives way to the water gradually out here. It is difficult to see where one ends and the other begins. Dense, swampy forest turns into marshy grassland with oak hammocks, which become ever smaller grassy islands, melting into the Gulf. There are no condos, no towering hotels, and no jetski and parasailing concessions out here. The only sign of human intrusion is this road and a few covered picnic tables at the end of it. On the way back, I stopped on the bridge. There was no sign declaring it, but this had to be Bird Creek. Thirty-five years before, Elvis had been here.

Out on the creek among the hammocks, I spotted someone paddling a canoe. He was wearing dark glasses, and from where I stood it looked like he had a tall shock of black hair combed straight back and long muttonchops.

DIRECTIONS: From Highway 19, turn west at Inglis on CR 40.

DON'T MISS: Dining at the Compleat Angler
ADDRESSES AND EVENTS: see page 198

CP1. Historic Ted Smallwood's Store, Chokoloskee

CP2. Rod and Gun Club, Everglades City

CP3. Sign on bait shop, Aripeka

CP4. 1916 Arcadia Drug Store, Arcadia

CP5. Park Avenue, Boca Grande

CP6. Crossed Palms Gallery, Bokeelia

CP7. 1859 Island Hotel, Cedar Key

CP8. Nell Lawrence King's Lawrence Grocery, Two Egg

CP9. Posey's Oyster Bar, St. Marks

CP10. Pioneer Cemetery, Islamorada

CP11. On the beach, Seaside

CP12. 1910 Masonic Lodge Building, Inverness

CP13. 1882 Wood & Swink Store and Post Office, Evinston

CP14. Marjorie Kinnan Rawlings' home, Cross Creek

CP15. 1893 J. P. Donnelly House, Mount Dora

CP16. Wheeler's Café, Arcadia

DUNNELLON

Population: 1,898

I'M NINETY MILES NORTH OF TAMPA, BUT I FEEL like I'm nine thousand miles away from all that traffic and congestion. Highway 484 winds through live oak–covered hills and brings me to Dunnellon, a pleasant and attractive north central Florida town located at the confluence of the Withlacoochee and Rainbow Rivers. With a population of fewer than nineteen hundred, it definitely qualifies as a small town.

It's Saturday and the first genuinely warm weekend of spring. I've stopped to walk across the sidewalk on the Highway 484 Bridge, which spans the Rainbow River on the east edge of town. A dozen people float sedately under the bridge on big black inner tubes. More are swimming or fishing on the other side. Standing on the bridge with me, a group of kids in bathing suits are yelling to their friends, who are floating underneath. One of them asks me, "Are you gonna jump?"

"No, I don't think so." It's about a twenty-five-foot drop from here to the crystal-clear water moving underneath us. I have to admit, I'm tempted for just a moment to climb over the railing and cannonball! Yahoo! "Is the water cold?" I ask the kids.

"Yeah, but you're glad for it when it's this hot out," one of them answers, and they all nod in agreement. "Why don't you find out for yourself?" They're egging me on.

"Nah, not today," I reply, the moment of temptation past.

Once a quiet citrus-farming community, Dunnellon became a mining boomtown overnight. In 1889, while digging a well in his backyard, Albertus Vogt discovered a vein of extraordinarily pure hard-rock phosphate. He took a sample to Ocala railroad man John F. Dunn, who promptly bought a half interest in the property owned by Albertus and his brother John. The Dunnellon Phosphate Company (named for Dunn's wife, Ellen) was born. One year later, the town of Dunnellon was incorporated. It promptly experienced the same transformation that Wild West towns had gone through during the Gold Rush. Schemers and scam artists smelled quick money and moved in. Saloons and brothels went up by the dozens. Saturday night street gunfights were commonplace. It was a slice of the Wild West in the Deep South, but it would not last forever.

The boom era and the lawlessness that accompanied it faded after the turn of the century. Then it disappeared completely with the onset of World War I and the consequential closing of the European markets for phosphate. Dunnellon returned to its quiet-community status. Around 1930, F. E. Hemphill and Frank Greene began to develop an area about three miles north of town that included the Rainbow Springs spring basin known then as Blue Springs. They built a lodge, a pavilion, and a dock for a glass-bottom boat. The springs changed hands a number of times over the next several decades. In the late 1960s, Holiday Inn and S & H Greenstamps jointly purchased the property and further developed it as a tourist theme park, complete with a monorail ride, glass-bottom boats, a paddle-wheel riverboat called the *Rainbow Queen*, and wild animal exhibits. But when I-75 was built, it bypassed Dunnellon to the east by twenty-two miles. Tourist traffic dried up, and the Rainbow Springs attraction closed its doors in 1974.

The community of Dunnellon knew that it had something special in Rainbow Springs, however. It is a first-magnitude spring with the fourth highest volume in Florida and a year-round water temperature of 73°. The Rainbow River's clear waters are filled with bass and bream. The spring is a wonderful natural resource that Dunnellon's residents could not stand to see go to waste. They wanted it to be accessible to the community, but they also wanted it to be preserved (and not as a theme park). Through the latter 1980s, a group of volunteers from Dunnellon and Citrus Springs and the Village of Rainbow Springs Garden Club worked diligently to restore the park, all at their own expense. Ultimately, they were able to convince the State of Florida to purchase the property in 1990 and turn it into a state park. In 1992, Rainbow Springs State Park opened on weekends only, with major financial and volunteer help from the community. In March 1995, it celebrated its grand opening as a full-time state park. To continue to maintain and

Rainbow Springs State Park

beautify the park, the original volunteer groups formed the Friends of Rainbow Springs State Park.

A sign at the entrance to Rainbow Springs State Park thanks Marion County residents for their contributions. When I pay my nominal admission fee, the park ranger tells me that I can rent tubes or canoes at K. P. Hole Park, just south of here. From the top of the bluff above the springs, I am looking straight down through the water to the bottom. The monorail, riverboat, and glass-bottom boats are long gone, but what's left is the natural beauty that has always been here.

DIRECTIONS: Take I-75 to the Highway 484/Belleview exit (Exit 341). Go west on Highway 484 into Dunnellon. From Dunnellon, go four miles north on Highway 41 to Rainbow Springs State Park.

DON'T MISS: Rainbow Springs State Park
ADDRESSES AND EVENTS: see page 198

OCKLAWAHA

Population: 1,000 (estimated)

ONE HOUR BEFORE DAWN ON THE MORNING OF January 16, 1935, residents of the sleepy, central Florida town of Ocklawaha simultaneously bolted upright in their beds, startled from their deep slumber by the rapid and continuous blasting of machine guns. It continued without pause for forty-five minutes, then went on sporadically for another five hours until FBI agents decided that notorious gangsters Ma Barker and her son Fred were surely dead.

Ocklawaha is a place far enough off the beaten path that if you were so inclined, you could hide away here for some time without being found. Arizona Clark "Ma" Barker, also known as Kate, must have had that same impression when she came here in November 1934 and rented a two-story, wood-frame house on the shore of Lake Weir under the alias Mrs. T. C. Blackburn.

Ocklawaha probably looked much the same then as it does now. It's a one-caution-light town on the north shore of Lake Weir, eight miles east of Belleview and about twenty miles southeast of Ocala. There's a new Lake Weir Chamber of Commerce office, the Lake Weir Community Building next door, a small city park, and the Lake Weir grocery, all on County Road 25, the main road through town. Turn down SE 135th Avenue to where it runs into Lake Weir and you'll find Gator Joe's Beach Bar and Grill in an old 1926 stilt building on the shore. They serve what I call "Cracker cuisine"—gator tail, frog's legs, and oysters as well as shrimp, grouper sandwiches, and burgers. Lake Weir is a popular summer water-skiing and fishing spot. Lake cabins and docks line the shore, and Gator Joe's is at the center of the activity.

Back out on County Road 25, heading west, look carefully for a small wooden sign that says "Harper's Place" at a dirt drive on the left. It's private property, so stop here. Tall grass and bushes shield the house where Ma and Fred Barker met their fate, except where the driveway meets the road. A sign says "No Trespassing" and, of course, I respect it. From here I'll get a distant glimpse of the house. It's a simple, white, wood-frame two-story with a screened porch downstairs—no different from a dozen other older houses along the shore at this end of Lake Weir. No different, except that sixty-odd years ago, the reign of one of history's most infamous gangs ended in a bloody gun battle here.

The Barker boys—Herman, Lloyd, Arthur (who was called "Doc"), and Fred—had always been bad eggs. As kids, they were bullies and thieves in their hometown of Webb City, Missouri, and later in Tulsa, Oklahoma. They spent most of their formative years in scrapes with the law. Ma, who as a child had seen in person and idolized Jesse James, not only tolerated these activities but encouraged them. She ultimately organized the Barkers into a criminal gang.

In 1922, police officers caught Lloyd during a post office hold up and sent him to Leavenworth. In 1927, the oldest brother, Herman, shot himself rather than be captured following a gun battle with police in Wichita, Kansas. Undaunted, the Barker gang continued its crime spree. The gang was joined by Alvin "Old Creepy" Karpis (nicknamed because of his constant menacing expression), a former Kansas State Penitentiary inmate and associate of Fred. For a while, bank robberies were their specialty, and they always left a trail of dead bodies behind—policemen, innocent bystanders, and sometimes fellow criminals. Then the Barkers figured out that there was more money in kidnapping than bank robbery when they abducted William Hamm Jr. of the Hamm Brewing Company in St. Paul, Minnesota. They collected $100,000 ransom for his release in June 1933. In January 1934, Fred and Old Creepy kidnapped wealthy St. Paul banker Edward Bremer. Bremer's family paid $200,000, and he was returned unharmed.

By now the Barker gang was at the top of the FBI's Most Wanted list. They were on the run. They even went so far as to have a doctor accomplice try to surgically alter their faces and scrape their fingers so their prints would be unrecognizable. The gang split and went in different directions to try to foil the FBI. That may have been the beginning of their downfall.

In January 1935 in Chicago, FBI agent Melvin Purvis caught Doc and sent him to Alcatraz. In Doc's apartment, agents found a map of Florida with a circle drawn around Ocala and Lake Weir. Ultimately, however, it was the Barkers' cruelty to animals that pinpointed their location for the FBI.

When Ma and Fred Barker (a.k.a. the Blackburns) first settled in Ocklawaha, they were considered friendly by the locals. They were regulars and big tippers at the bar. But before long, boredom got the best of Fred, and he took to shooting at ducks on Lake Weir with his machine gun. This did not set well with the locals. When Fred let it be known that he wanted to hunt down "Old Joe," a legendary but harmless old alligator that lived in the lake, the locals were enraged, and word of his intentions spread. His description matched one given by the FBI, and in the early morning of January 16, fourteen agents surrounded the house.

Chief Agent E. J. Connelly announced, "We're from the Department of Justice. Come out one at a time."

Ma barker yelled, "All right, Freddie! Go ahead!" and the Barkers opened fire. FBI agents fired over fifteen hundred rounds of bullets into the house in three quarters of an hour and then continued to shoot through the windows intermittently for several more hours. When they finally went inside, they found Ma and Fred dead on the floor of the bullet-ridden upstairs bedroom. They also found an arsenal of rifles, machine guns, pistols, and ammunition. Ma still clutched her machine gun in her hands.

A year later, J. Edgar Hoover caught up with Alvin Karpis in New Orleans. Karpis spent thirty-two years in prison. Ten years after his release, he died of an overdose of pills. Lloyd Barker served a twenty-five-year sentence and then was shot by his wife two years after his release. In 1939, Doc Barker attempted to escape from Alcatraz. He made it over the walls and was standing on the shore of the island when guards fatally shot him.

The town of Ocklawaha puts on an annual Ma Barker Festival the second weekend in January. Local police do a reenactment of the shootout, and there's lots of food and live entertainment.

DIRECTIONS: From Highway 441, south of Ocala, turn east at Belleview on CR 25.

DON'T MISS: Well, don't blink or you'll miss Ocklawaha
ADDRESSES AND EVENTS: see page 198

CASSADAGA AND LAKE HELEN

Population: Cassadaga 200 (estimated);
Lake Helen 2,743

ONE HUNDRED TWENTY YEARS AGO, GEORGE COLBY was financially destitute and in poor health. However, by all accounts, he was thought to be spiritually wealthy. Colby claimed that, during a séance, an Indian spirit guide named Seneca had instructed him to take a journey south. He would build a community where other spiritualists could learn, live, and teach. First, he must go by way of Wisconsin. In Wisconsin, Colby met T. D. Giddings. In another séance, Seneca directed the two of them specifically to go to Florida. Colby and Giddings' family settled on a lake in wild central Florida that Colby claimed he had envisioned in the séance. In 1880, he built a home and filed for homestead on seventy-four and a half acres. Homestead was granted four years later, but Colby didn't stay. He set out across the country to lecture and hold séances. It was not until 1894 that a group from New York approached George Colby about organizing the Southern Cassadaga Spiritualist Camp Meeting Association. In January 1895, he deeded thirty-five acres of his property to the Association, and the community of **Cassadaga** was born. They held their first camp meeting the following month in Colby's home.

Cassadaga must have been at least somewhat financially successful, although that was not its purpose. George Colby was able to live there for most of the balance of his life as the town's main spiritual advisor. Early writings about nearby Lake Helen describe T. D. Giddings' house as prominent and the first to have "real glass windows."

Originally, Cassadaga was just a winter retreat for psychics from up north. As more people arrived around the turn of the century, the Association began leasing plots of land to them to build their own homes on. This owned-house-on-leased-land arrangement still exists with most of the homeowners today. All of the town's residents, then and now, are spiritualists, and many are mediums or psychics. Cassadaga's current fifty-seven acres have been designated a historic district on the National Register of Historic Places.

The Association defines a spiritualist as "one who believes, as the basis of his or her religion, in the communication of this and the spirit world by means of mediumship, and who endeavors to mold his or her character and conduct in accordance with the highest teachings derived from such communion." Mediums, of course, are those who communicate with the spirit world.

If reading your horoscope in the newspaper just isn't telling you enough, then maybe a trip to Cassadaga is in order. By arrangement with the reception desk at the Cassadaga Hotel and for $42 (as of this writing), anyone can spend thirty minutes with one of the on-duty psychics. Depending on the psychic's best-developed abilities, he or she will divine your future by reading Tarot cards, your palm, or your aura. Psychics may also interpret your dreams; in a longer session, some will do a past-life regression.

The current two-story Cassadaga Hotel was built in 1928 (the original burned in a fire in 1926) and is the town's centerpiece. If you're not interested in whether you'll soon become famous or in how you'll meet the spouse of your dreams, you can have a sandwich in the Lost In Time Café in the hotel lobby. Or visit the Cassadaga Camp Bookstore and Gift Shop, located across the street in the 1905 Andrew Jackson Davis Building. The bookstore has a good selection of new-age CDs. For something sweet, walk a half block up Stevens Street to the old Cassadaga Grocery Store, which is not really a grocery store. It's a sandwich and ice cream café. Try the homemade Toll House cookie ice cream sandwich.

My favorite pastime is walking around the narrow streets of Cassadaga and looking at the houses. Some are cute, gingerbready, and brightly painted, while others are obscured by overgrown vines and overhanging Spanish moss and are creepy. All have a shingle hanging out front that typically reads, "Dr. (or Reverend) So-and-so, Certified (or Registered) Medium; Palmistry, Tarot, Spiritual Guidance. Readings by appointment only."

Drive out of Cassadaga on County Road 4139 (Cassadaga Road), then turn right on Kicklighter to find Clauser's Inn Bed & Breakfast. Tom and Marge Clauser opened their bed and breakfast on New Year's Day in 1990 with just two rooms. Word of the charming country

Cassadaga Hotel

Stevens Street, Cassadaga

Victorian house—and Marge's marvelous cooking—spread fast. In 1994, they built a separate Carriage House behind the original house, adding six more rooms and something out of the ordinary for a bed and breakfast: an English pub, which they call Sherlock's. Clauser's is listed on the National Register of Historic Places as the Ann C. Stevens House, built circa 1895. The property was part of George Colby's original homestead. He sold it to Stevens, a fellow spiritualist and farm owner from Michigan. Stevens Street in Cassadaga is named for her.

The Clausers have done an excellent job of restoring the three-story Victorian house. Outside, the broad, wraparound porch invites you to sit and soak up the serenity in one of its many rocking chairs. Inside, the front sitting room, the dining room, and especially the kitchen are decorated to give the place a warm, country-home feeling. A gallery of pictures hangs on one wall, old family photos from both sides of Marge and Tom's family. One is of Gen. George Armstrong Custer, Tom's great granduncle. Each of the eight rooms has an individual theme—from Pennsylvania Dutch to Colonial America to old-Florida. My favorite of all of them is the Laredo Room. It's right out of an old *Bonanza* set. Horseshoes, a bullwhip, and a ten-gallon hat hang on the wall. It has wooden barrels for nightstands and a king-size bed frame made from logs to match the walls.

A little further down the road, County Road 4139 leads into the

Home on Euclid Avenue, Lake Helen

town of **Lake Helen,** whose historic district, particularly Euclid Avenue, has a number of beautifully restored turn-of-the-century homes. The standout is a majestic, three-story Victorian plantation home called Edgewood at 214 Euclid Avenue. Cincinnati architect and builder John Porter Mace brought his family to Lake Helen in 1885. He built Edgewood as their home and designed and built many of the other homes in Lake Helen as well. An industrious fellow and a major contributor to Lake Helen's development, Mace was the town's first mayor, owned a lumberyard and sawmill, and was one of the largest orange growers and packers in the county. The brand name for his oranges was Edgewood.

DIRECTIONS: From I-4, take the Orange City/Blue Springs/Cassadaga/Highway 472 exit (Exit 54). Go northeast 1/3 mile on Highway 472 to CR 4101. Go right for a couple hundred yards, then turn right again at CR 4139/Cassadaga Road and follow it back across the I-4 overpass into Cassadaga. Continue on CR 4139/Macy Avenue another mile into Lake Helen.

DON'T MISS: A stroll through the neighborhood streets of Cassadaga
ADDRESSES AND EVENTS: see page 198–199

MOUNT DORA

Population: 9,418

IN MOST NATIVE FLORIDIANS' MINDS, MOUNT DORA, at 184 feet above sea level, qualifies as a mountain, although it doesn't come close to Florida's highest point. That would be 345-foot-high Britton Hill at Lakewood Park near Paxton, Florida, close to the Alabama state line. Britton Hill appears relatively flat, but Mount Dora looks mountainous, or at least very hilly.

Downtown Mount Dora is storybook picturesque, with tree-lined streets, Victorian street lamps, and a multitude of parks, antiques shops, galleries, and restaurants. It would fit in nicely in New England. The numbered avenues, running east to west, roll steeply down to Lake Dora. Mount Dora bustles with activity. Although it's a wonderful place to retire, I can't call it a retirement town. There's just too much going on. The list of festivals and events is lengthy: an exotic and antique automobile festival in February; the annual art festival in February; an antique boat show in March; and the famous bicycle festival in October. The entire month of December is one long Christmas festival, with a lighted boat parade, street parades, and elaborate town decorations and lighting.

Your first stop in this enchanting town should be the Mount Dora Area Chamber of Commerce, where you'll find maps and lists of antiques shops, restaurants, and other attractions. It's located in the old train depot at Alexander Street and Third Avenue. The railroad brought people to Mount Dora just as it had to other small towns in Florida. Track was laid from Sanford north to Mount Dora in 1887. The small, original depot was replaced in 1915 by the current, larger structure. In 1973, the Seaboard Coastline Railroad agreed to lease it to the

Chamber for one dollar per year.

The Lakeside Inn, Mount Dora's oldest standing structure, is one block from the train depot. The inn was built in 1883 and is listed on the National Register of Historic Places. Originally a ten-room hotel named The Alexander House, it was the joint project of key Mount Dora developers James Alexander, John MacDonald, and J. P. Donnelly. When they sold it in 1893, the name changed to Lake House. When it changed hands again in 1933, it became the Lakeside Inn. During the 1920s and '30s, the inn was the place to be in Mount Dora. One historical highlight of note is that in the winter of 1930, Calvin Coolidge came to the inn for an extended sabbatical with his wife following his just-completed term as president. During his stay, he dedicated the newly completed Gables and Terrace Wings.

James Barggren and Richard Dempsey bought the Lakeside Inn in 1992, and they have restored it to its 1920s–30s heyday style. With the main building and two wings, the inn has eighty-eight rooms, a lounge, a restaurant, tennis courts, a pool, and a dock on the lake. Perhaps the most enjoyable activity, though, is sitting in one of the rocking chairs on the main lodge's expansive veranda, sipping iced tea and soaking up the view across placid Lake Dora.

The most interesting and ornate house in Mount Dora is, without question, the Donnelly House at the uphill end of Donnelly Street between Fifth and Sixth Avenues. The Masonic Lodge currently owns it so you can't get inside, but the outside is a grand example of Queen

Lakeside Inn

The Donnelley House

Odom's Interiors

Anne Victorian style. In Donnelly's day—the late 1800s to early 1900s—it was referred to as the "gingerbread house." Donnelly had homesteaded 160 acres adjacent to property owned by Annie Stone, one of the earliest homesteaders. In 1881, the two married and began the development of what is now downtown Mount Dora. They built their gingerbread house in 1893. Donnelly, one of Mount Dora's most prominent citizens, went on to be the town's first mayor in 1910. In 1924, he sold the large tract of land across the street from his house to the city for a park named in honor of his wife.

Arts and crafts and antiques shoppers will find more than enough variety and quantity to keep them busy in the several-block downtown district. Oliver's Twist Antiques on Donnelly Street has an extensive inventory of antique estate furniture and an interesting collection of antique postcards dating back to the 1930s. Piece of Mine and Eclectic Avenue both specialize in exotic sculpture and art from around the world. At 5th Avenue Stained Glass, in the old Simpson Hotel building on 5th Avenue (of course), Renee Graham sells antique stained-glass windows that she imports from England. Most come from country houses built in the 1930s, but some date back to before the turn of the twentieth century. A couple of doors down you'll find Dickens-Reed Bookshop, a terrific independent bookstore. Piglet's Pantry at the corner of Donnelly and 4th has gourmet pet treats and pet toys. Some of the best people treats can be found a half block down 4th at a gift and baked-goods shop called The Amish Cupboard and Country Stuff. Odom's Interiors at Alexander and 4th is a fascinating place. It occupies a genuine Sears and Roebuck mail-order house, built here in 1928. Stanton Childs, a furniture designer from New York, lived here and donated the land across the street to the city for a park.

If you've worked up an appetite from shopping, there are plenty of options. Park Bench, The Palm Tree Grille, and The Gables (try their Maryland crab cakes) are three fine restaurants. Try Le Cremerie on Donnelly for ice cream or coffee. My favorite place for lunch has to be the Windsor Rose English Tea Room on 4th Avenue. British royalty memorabilia decorate the walls, and music reminiscent of the 1940s plays in the background. The menu features strictly authentic British fare. My favorite is the cottage pie, a sort of casserole made with mashed potatoes, ground beef, and vegetables topped with brown gravy.

Hike down Donnelly Street south to its lakeside end and you'll find

*Mount Dora lawn
bowling*

Evans Park. Next to the park are Mount Dora's lawn-bowling courts. Lawn bowling is a very old Scottish and English game, still popular in English-speaking countries like Australia, New Zealand, and, of course, Great Britain. The Mount Dora Lawn Bowling Club has been in existence since 1928 and is the largest in the United States.

A game of finesse and strategy, lawn bowling has strict rules. In tournaments, everyone wears white. The bowls—not balls—are slightly flattened on two sides so they can be rolled in a curving path, if that is the bowler's intention. The basic object of the game is for players to bowl as closely as possible to a smaller, white jack ball at the opposite end of the court. Sometimes other players' bowls are blocking the direct path, hence the need for a curved trajectory.

DIRECTIONS: Twenty-nine miles north of Orlando on Highway 441.

DON'T MISS: The Windsor Rose English Tea Room
ADDRESSES AND EVENTS: see page 199–200

INVERNESS

Population: 6,789

THE ROUGH-AND-READY TOMPKINS BROTHERS, post–Civil War Confederate soldiers, settled here in 1868. They called it Tompkinsville. Records show that the name changed to Inverness in 1889. Local legend claims that an emigrant Scotsman (whose name no one can recall) became homesick while standing on the banks of Lake Tsala Apopka (adjacent to Tompkinsville/Inverness). It reminded him of the lake country near his home in Inverness, Scotland. At least one report claims that the Scotsman was one of the many phosphate-boom speculators who swarmed to north-central Florida in the late 1880s and early 1890s and that he offered to donate two thousand dollars toward the construction of a new courthouse if the name of the town was changed.

In 1887, the newly formed Citrus County had designated the nearby town of Mannfield as the temporary county seat. Four years later, a county election decided that Inverness would be the permanent county seat—much to the disappointment of the residents of Mannfield and to the consternation of Senator Austin S. Mann, who developed Mannfield. W. C. Zimmerman (then clerk of the circuit court) refused to deliver the county records to their new location and also to vacate the old Mannfield office. He sat at his desk while the entire office was removed from around him and loaded on a wagon. Finally, the sheriff and a contingent of deputies loaded Zimmerman, still in his chair, onto the wagon along with his desk and boxes of records and transported everything to the new offices in Inverness. Accounts I have read say that Zimmerman continued to record minutes throughout the trip. Inverness went on to become a center of commerce while Mannfield became a ghost town. Zimmerman later became the Citrus County Superintendent of Schools.

At first, Inverness townsfolk feared that the widening of US Highway 41 in 1993—and the consequential bypass of their downtown Main Street—would be the equivalent of cutting off the blood supply to a limb. Happily, the opposite happened. Thanks to a committee of local business people, instead of succumbing to a withering death, downtown Inverness got an injection of new life. Its one-block-long Main Street— the historic Citrus County Courthouse marking its east end and the twenty-foot-tall Bank of Inverness clock at its west end—is now a vibrant district with restaurants, galleries, and shops.

Main Street's restaurants—Stumpknocker's, Angelo's Pizzeria, and Coach's—offer a variety of dining options. Among the assortment of shops are Vanishing Breeds (a gift shop and boutique with an endangered animals theme), Ritzy Rags and Glitzy Jewels, Country at Home (bears and candles), At Wick's End (candles and homemade soaps), and Sandy Bottom Bayou (restored and antique furniture).

Gas lantern–style street lights blend well with Main Street's restored buildings and storefronts. The brick, three-story, neoclassical-revival Masonic Lodge Building at the corner of Main and Pine Streets was considered a skyscraper when it was constructed (for $17,285) in 1910. The Masons of Lodge #18 used the third floor and leased the first floor to retail shops and the second floor to a dance and theater production group. Today the restored building once again has retail shops downstairs. The Citrus County Board of County Commissioners, a real estate office, and a law firm occupy the upper floors.

The old yellow-brick 1912 Citrus County Courthouse, which replaced the original 1892 wood structure, has been immaculately restored under the supervision of the Citrus County Historical Society. The process, completed in October 2000, took eight years and $2.5 million. They now call it the Citrus County Heritage Museum. I originally visited the courthouse in 1997 while the restoration was still taking place, and to see the finished result now is astounding. Downstairs rooms that previously housed the offices of tax collectors, judges, and clerks of the court are now a gallery portraying local history, an exhibit of pre- and early history artifacts, and a museum store with books and photo reprints. The most impressive room, however, is the old court-

room, which occupies the entire second floor. Architects used old photographs to accurately reconstruct details throughout the building, but
for the courtroom they watched old reels of the 1961 Elvis Presley
movie *Follow That Dream*. The closing courthouse scene was filmed in
the second-floor courtroom, and everyone saw what the room looked
like then. (Much of the movie was also filmed in Yankeetown. For more
information, see the Yankeetown chapter.)

Many of Inverness' other buildings and houses from its prosperous
turn-of-the-century era are still in use. Some have been restored. One of
the most impeccable restorations I've seen in all my small-town research is
Inverness' Citrus High School, now the administration building for Citrus
Memorial Hospital. This red-brick, two-story building, with a bell tower
over its entrance, was originally built in 1911 and restored in 1992. Photos
on the corridor walls chronicle the thorough reconstruction.

Some other interesting and historic structures are the 1910 Clark
House at 314 West Main Street, now a Coldwell Banker Real Estate
office; the 1901 Carter House at 301 West Main Street, with its hexagonal corner gazebo, now offices of the *Citrus Times* (an edition of the *St.
Petersburg Times*); and the 1900 Hicks House at the corner of Tompkins
Street and Osceola Avenue. Robert Hicks built this unusual octagonal
house to withstand hurricanes, and it is still in the Hicks family.

My favorite Inverness historic building is the Crown Hotel. This
white, three-story, wooden structure, with burgundy canvas awnings
over its windows, reminds me of a Scottish country club. But the now-
dignified inn had humble beginnings. The Crown began life as a general store when Alf, one of the Tompkins brothers, gave his brother-in-law,
Francis Dampier, property on which to build a store. Dampier built the
store on one side of the street and his home on the other side. Sometime
around 1900, Dampier moved his store from Bay Street to Main Street,
and in 1907 he turned it into a boarding house called the Orange Hotel.
Ten years after that, he sold it to a New York hotel syndicate, which
moved it again in 1926, this time around the corner to Seminole
Avenue, its present location.

In conjunction with the move, the New York group performed what
must have been an amazing feat of construction in its day: They built an
entirely new bottom floor, then hoisted the original two-story building
up into the air and placed it on top of the new first floor to make a
three-story hotel, which they named the Colonial.

The very regal and very British Crown Hotel in Inverness.

The Colonial was a popular place for a number of decades, but by the 1970s it had fallen into serious disrepair. It had recently been condemned when, in 1979, Reg Brealy came to Inverness, representing the British company Epicure Holdings. The company had sent Brealy to look at another piece of property, but he convinced them that the Colonial was the real diamond in the rough. They bought it for a reported $100,000 and spent the next year and a half (and an additional $2 million) completely restoring it in fine English-residence style. Epicure Holdings renamed the structure the Crown Hotel and also built a new restaurant and kitchen and added a swimming pool.

The Crown is everything a British inn should be: regal, stately, and elegant, with an interior decorated in forest green, burgundy, and, of course, royal blue. A crystal chandelier hangs from the ceiling in the lobby atrium. A wide, curving, one-piece, floating staircase sweeps around the chandelier up to the second-floor landing. Lithographs depicting British countryside hunting scenes hang from hallway walls. Beneath the stairs, a glass case displays an exact replica of the Crown jewels. Epicure Holdings purchased the set from one of the few British companies licensed to reproduce the gems.

At one time, the hotel even had its own authentic 1909 double-decker bus, purchased at an auction in London. It was an Inverness landmark that sat parked in front of the Crown for many years. Ownership of the Crown has changed hands several times since its restoration, but it still retains its decidedly British air, as do its two restaurants, Churchill's and The Fox and Hound.

The forty-six-mile-long Withlacoochee State Trail (which runs roughly from Trilby in the south to Dunnellon in the north) was one of Florida's first "Rails to Trails" projects. The state bought the rail right-of-way, which was no longer in use, and converted it into a state park trail. It comes to its approximate two-thirds point in Inverness and passes through just a couple of blocks north of the Crown Hotel.

I can best summarize Inverness as a picturesque and historic small town with a touch of old-world charm and class.

DIRECTIONS: Take US Highway 41 north from Brooksville.

DON'T MISS: The Crown Hotel and the Courthouse Museum
ADDRESSES AND EVENTS: see page 200–201

FLORAL CITY, PINEOLA, ISTACHATTA,

AND

NOBLETON

Population: Floral City 4,989; Istachatta 93; Pineola and Nobleton, fewer than 100 combined (estimated)

EARLY SETTLER HUGH BOYLAND MUST HAVE BEEN captivated by the profusion of wildflowers when he suggested the name **Floral City** for this picturesque village, which was officially laid out in 1883. The following year, Boyland contributed something else to the town: oak trees, which he planted in rows on each side of Orange Avenue (County Road 48). Over the past century, those trees have grown tall and wide and have crossed over the top of Orange Avenue, forming a quarter-mile-long tunnel known as the "Avenue of Oaks."

Like nearly everyone who passes through here, I have to stop at the crest of the hill on East Orange Avenue and take some pictures. The branches of these grand oaks reach clear across the road to intertwine with one another. I can't tell where branches from the south side end and those from the north side begin.

Aroostook Avenue, with its own rows of oak trees, forks diagonally northeast from here and dead-ends at the shores of Lake Tsala Apopka. This was a busy steamboat port from which oranges, along with lumber and the occasional passenger, could be shipped via the newly completed (in 1884) Orange State Canal down the Withlacoochee River to the railhead at Lake Panasoffkee. Aroostook Avenue was Floral City's original Main Street until the big freeze of 1894–1895 killed the area's citrus industry and ended the steamboat business. Fortunately, right around the same time, phosphate was discovered nearby. Mines opened up, and Floral City had a new industry.

This quaint town has an impressive collection of historic homes and buildings, some restored but most simply well preserved. Many were built during the phosphate boom (1890s–1910s), when Floral City's population swelled briefly to more than ten thousand because of the influx of transient mine workers. At least one house predates that era: The Formy-Duval House, at 7801 Old Floral City Road (which runs north and south a couple of blocks east of Highway 41), was built in 1865. It is the oldest house still standing in the area. John Paul Formy-Duval was a cotton, sugarcane, and citrus farmer who owned vast tracts of land surrounding the southern end of Lake Tsala Apopka. Some of his land, totaling 342 acres, would eventually become Floral City.

The 1894 D. A. Tooke House, at 8560 Orange Avenue, and the 1910 J. T. Love House, next door at 8580 Orange Avenue, are two good examples of the Queen Anne Victorian architectural style. Both are large, one-story homes with twin, steep-roofed gables. The simple wood-frame Floral City Methodist Church, at 8508 Marvin Street (a block north of Orange Avenue), has been in continuous use since its construction in 1884. The Cracker Victorian–style W. C. Zimmerman House, at 8441 East Orange Avenue, was built in 1890. (See Inverness chapter about W. C. Zimmerman.) The cedar shingle–sided Soloman Moon House, at 8860 East Orange Avenue, was built in 1893. The 1904 William H. Dunn House, at 8050 South Bedford Road (on the west side of Highway 41 and several blocks south of Orange Avenue), is the boyhood home of well-known Florida historian Hampton Dunn. Hampton's nephew and his nephew's wife now live in the house.

The two-story 1889 Commercial Hotel (also called the Magnolia Hotel) at 8375 East Orange Avenue—with its full-width front porch, leaded stained-glass windows, and triple-gabled roof—was originally the home of James Baker, son-in-law of John Paul Formy-Duval. Baker was one of the principal developers of Floral City. The house was relocated from two blocks away in 1895 and converted into an elegant hotel. It's now a private residence.

Floral City's largest business is citrus grower Ferris Groves. Doc Ferris started his orange grove business in 1927, when he took over property on Duval Island in Lake Tsala Apopka, on which his father had originally intended to build a golf course. Ferris reintroduced citrus to the area after its forty-year absence. In 1940, Ferris built a packing plant and a roadside fruit stand on Highway 41 just north of Orange Avenue. In 1955, he built a permanent fruit store and gift shop that still operates today. It is reminiscent of the many tourist shops that sprang up in the 1950s and '60s along Florida thoroughfares. After another hard freeze in the mid-1980s, the folks at Ferris Groves changed their focus to strawberries, for which they are famous today.

A note of Floral City trivia: A few of the town's residents were relatives of famous people. Doc Ferris was the grandnephew of George Washington Gale Ferris, who invented the Ferris wheel and introduced it at the 1893 Chicago World's Fair. One of Floral City's early (1880s) orange grove farmers, Jacob Clemens, was the cousin of Samuel Clemens (Mark Twain). Floral City resident Robert Dillinger (by all accounts, a mild-mannered fellow) was cousin to notorious 1930s' gangster John Dillinger. Floral City's best-known native was Hampton Dunn, a longtime Tampa resident. When Mr. Dunn passed away in February 2002, Florida lost one of its finest historians (and one of my favorite resources for Florida history). No one could bring Florida's past to life like Hampton Dunn.

This book is supposed to be about small towns, but once in a while the roads that run between them are worth mentioning. Take Orange Avenue east out of Floral City, then turn south onto Istachatta Road (County Road 39). Istachatta Road winds through some of the most scenic rolling hills, oak hammocks, and horse farms in the state. This is one of Florida's best top-down roadster roads. The pavement snakes along beneath overhanging oaks past horse farms and pastureland for seven miles. It parallels and crisscrosses the Withlacoochee State Trail. Near its south end, it eases into quiet **Pineola**, made up of a handful of residences and an old cemetery next to the New Hope United Methodist Church, one of the oldest churches in this area. Church founders built the original New Hope Church out of logs on this site in 1830, then replaced it with a wood-frame structure following a fire in 1886. In 1940, the congregation built the current church, reusing much of the lumber from the 1886 building. Some of the hand-hewn pews are from the original 1830 church. New Hope's annual October Homecoming draws a good-size crowd of past parishioners from around the state.

Just past Pineola is **Istachatta**. The name has been variously interpreted as Creek Indian for "red man" and "man's river crossing." There was a ferry crossing here on the Withlacoochee River in the 1800s that was replaced by an iron bridge in 1910 (which is no longer there). Istachatta has a community park, a library, a tiny post office, and the

Istachatta General Store. This is a real general store, not one done up for tourists. The shelves are filled with staples—canned goods, flour, butter, milk, and eggs. A handwritten sign on the wall reads, "Boiled Peanuts $1.99 a Qt." The store also has three tables and serves breakfast and lunch. I'm kind of partial to the cheeseburger.

Continuing south then east on Lake Lindsey Road (County Road 476) for about a mile and a half brings you to **Nobleton**, at the crossing of the Withlacoochee River. The Nobleton Boat Rental Outpost, on the north side of the highway, rents canoes, kayaks, and pontoon boats and gives airboat rides. That's one half of Nobleton. The other half is the Riverside Restaurant & Bar, on the south side of the highway.

These four communities—three so tiny that each has fewer than a hundred residents—still retain much of the old-Florida flavor, and I hope that never changes.

DIRECTIONS: Floral City: Take US Highway 41 north from Brooksville to Floral City.
Pineola and Istachatta: Take CR 48 east to CR 39 and go south.
Nobleton: Continue south and then east on CR 476.

DON'T MISS: A drive down Istachatta Road
ADDRESSES AND EVENTS: see page 201

ARIPEKA,
BAYPORT,
CHASSAHOWITZKA,
AND OZELLO

*Population: Aripeka 200
(estimated); Chassahowitzka
300 (estimated); Bayport 36;
Ozello 300 (estimated)*

"USELESS 19"—THAT'S WHAT DRIVERS HAVE DUBBED the stretch of US Highway 19 from Clearwater north. It has been widened and overpasses have been built at crossroads, but it is still a frustrating experience to travel on this main Pinellas County/Pasco County artery—an artery that could use an angioplasty, in my opinion. It's not just the traffic that exasperates me; it's also the tacky suburban clutter that sprouts up alongside the highway, like the crabgrass that invades my front yard.

Not until well past Hudson does US 19 become "useful" again. Five miles further north, I turn west down Pasco County Road 595/Aripeka Road. The contrast is dramatic. Pastureland replaces parking lots and gives way to piney woods and brackish swamps as I approach the small, coastal port community of **Aripeka**, called Gulf Key when it was first settled in 1886. Back then, visitors rode the *Governor Stafford* passenger steamer here for fishing and recreation. They stayed at the Osawaw Inn (now gone), built by the Aripeka Saw Mill Company. Gulf Key adopted its new name from the company. Aripeka is most likely a slight variation on Arpeika, a Miccosukee Seminole chief who also went by the unlikely name of Sam Jones. In 1835, just prior to the Second Seminole War, then-Governor Andrew Jackson mandated that all Seminole Indians be removed from Florida and sent to reservations out West. Chief Arpeika was one of eight tribe leaders who refused to relocate their people. Instead, they fled south to the Everglades and established Sam Jones Old Town near present-day Fort Lauderdale. An alternate claim is that Aripeka is a mispronunciation of another Seminole leader's name, Apayaka.

Thankfully, Aripeka's rate of growth has been nominal over the past one hundred plus years. It is still a quiet fishing enclave. A few stilt fishing shacks appear on my right as the road slows at a sharp S-turn before bridging the south fork and then the north fork of Hammock Creek. A small bait-and-tackle and general store sits between the bridges and backs up to the north fork. The faded wooden sign on the front depicts a palm tree, beach, and sunset paradise. It reads "Aripeka, Fla. 5.9 miles from Heaven." Inside, fishing lures, leaders, rods and reels, bait buckets, and long-billed hats hang on racks and occupy shelves alongside groceries. I asked the manager, "What is it that's five point nine miles away?" He replied, "Five point nine miles to the best fishing spot in the Gulf, but I'm not saying in which direction."

Outside, I watched fishermen toss cast nets off the side of the closest bridge. This is the heart of Aripeka. No motels. No restaurants. Just a quiet place to cast a net or drop a line and soak up the beautiful, natural Gulf coast scenery. From here west, Hammock Creek spills out across a sawgrass delta and into the Gulf of Mexico. The view is idyllic and should be even more so at sunset. If Heaven is 5.9 miles out there somewhere, then this must be the Pearly Gates.

County Road 595 continues north from Aripeka and follows the shoreline for a couple of miles. It's difficult to tell where the sawgrass ends and the Gulf begins. Turn west on Highway 50, which leads to Bayport on a marshy point at the mouth of the Weeki Wachee River. The road ends at a picturesque park with a boat ramp.

Bayport was a lumber, cotton, and supplies port during the Civil War. Like many other small Gulf Coast ports, Bayport became vital after the Union's East Gulf Blockading Squadron succeeded in cutting off the larger ports. By 1864, Union troops felt that Bayport had become significant enough to invade it too. For twenty years after the war ended, Bayport was a bustling town and the area's busiest port. Regularly scheduled wagon runs transported goods between here and Brooksville, but in 1885 rail service came to Brooksville, and Bayport's usefulness declined rapidly. Nothing remains of the town today, but the park and boat ramp are popular put-in spots for the Weeki Wachee River.

Back out on US 19, continue north and pass D.O.T. signs that warn drivers to watch for bears crossing. This is one of the few remaining habitats for Florida black bears. Just north of the Hernando–Citrus County line, Miss Maggie Road turns west off of US 19 and winds down to **Chassahowitzka** (Timucuan Indian for "pumpkin place"). It ends at the Chassahowitzka River Campground and Recreational Area, the best place to rent canoes or kayaks to explore the Chassahowitzka National Wildlife Refuge. The Refuge encompasses more than thirty thousand acres of brackish marsh and salt bays, stretching from Raccoon Point north to the mouth of the Homosassa River. It's home to several hundred species of birds, including a variety of herons, pelicans, ducks, ospreys, and even bald eagles. Manatees, green sea turtles, deer, and a small population of black bears live here as well.

Overnighters will want to stay at the Chassahowitzka Hotel, just up the road. David and Kim Strickland opened the current version in 2000, but it was David's grandparents, Ben and Eliza Smith, who built the original on this same site in 1910.

Just north of Homosassa, I turn west on Citrus County 494/West Ozello Trail. For a mile or so, the road winds through a swampy forest. There's no shoulder. The palmetto scrub grows wild right up to the edge of the road. Intermittently, as I near the coast, the road opens up to sawgrass savannas dotted with cedar bay heads. The community of **Ozello** (the westernmost in Citrus County) is technically on an island, separated from the mainland by tributaries of the St. Martin River, Salt Creek, and Greenleaf Bay. A million water passageways crosshatch this nether land, looking like varicose veins on the map. Airboats are the transport of choice here.

Until 1955, Ozello Trail was an oyster-shell path with palmetto logs bridging the swampy sections. It frequently flooded out, but this was no deterrent to the local residents, who were accustomed to getting around by boat. From 1880 until 1943, Ozello's children daily paddled rowboats and canoes to their one-room schoolhouse on one of the many tiny hammocks in the bay just south of Ozello. They called it the Isle of Knowledge. The island is still there (south off the end of John Brown Road), but, unfortunately, the schoolhouse is gone.

Ozello Trail ends at the edge of the open Gulf and at Peck's Old Port Cove Seafood Restaurant and Blue Crab Farm. Calvin Peck has been harvesting blue crabs in specially constructed tanks behind his restaurant since 1982. Around back, I get to survey his operation. Hundreds of blue crabs fill fourteen tanks. One of the chefs is scooping up a bucketful of the scrambling critters.

On my original visit to Peck's in 1998, I had devoured a heaping, steaming plate of garlic crabs. On a recent return visit, I tried to exercise more culinary control and just ordered the fried grouper fingers. They were fresh, delicious, and plentiful. They came with coleslaw, fries, and the requisite hush puppies. I noticed a "For Sale" sign alongside the building and asked my waitress if Calvin was retiring. "Not a chance. He put that sign up five years ago, and this place is still bustling, especially on weekends," she replied. Back up the road a ways, I found the Wench's Brew Restaurant had changed its name to Captain Hook's, but the menu is the same fresh assortment of seafood, and you can still park your boat at their dock out back.

I was pleased to find that little else has changed in Ozello. It still attracts a few artists who have opened studios, none more eclectic than Harpozello Nature Studios run by Harpo Leech.

DIRECTIONS: Five miles north of Hudson, take CR 595 west off US 19 to Aripeka. Continue north from Aripeka on CR 595 to Highway 50 and go west to Bayport. Go west on Miss Maggie Drive off US 19, just north of the Citrus/Hernando County line, to Chassahowitzka. Go west on Citrus County 494/West Ozello Trail off US 19 between Homosassa and Crystal River to Ozello.

DON'T MISS: Peck's Old Port Cove Seafood Restaurant and Blue Crab Farm

ADDRESSES AND EVENTS: see page 201–202

WEBSTER

Population: 805

I CAN SURE TELL IT'S MONDAY. I'M HEADING NORTH on Highway 471, and although I'm still four miles south of Webster, I'm already seeing all the indications that today is flea market day. Garage sale signs, roadside stands, and vendors working out of the backs of vans and pickups line the highway.

Every Monday, the Sumter County Farmer's Market in Webster hosts Florida's largest and probably oldest flea market. Sumter County has always had an agricultural-based economy. Citrus was big here prior to the Great Freeze of 1894. After that, peppers, cucumbers, cabbage, lettuce, beans, and other vegetables became the staple crops. In the early 1900s, Webster was known as the "Cucumber Capital." In 1937, a group of local farmers formed a co-op and, without state funding or financial help from the county, built a market in the middle of Webster from which to auction their produce. The farmers built the facility themselves, harvesting cypress trees from nearby swamp lands and using mules to drag out the lumber. The farmer's market was then and remains today a not-for-profit operation. It is still owned and operated by local agricultural business people.

Over the decades, the market evolved along with changes in local farming trends. A cattle auction (now the second largest in Florida) replaced the vegetable auction, and people began to sell other items out of the empty produce stalls. These days the cattle auction takes place on Tuesdays, the flea market on Mondays. When I inquire at the office about the flea market's schedule, a friendly lady behind the counter cheerfully gives me what must be her standard answer: "Fifty-two weeks a year, unless Christmas comes on a Monday."

The enormous, forty-acre facility overwhelms me from the minute I walk through the market's gates. A dozen roofed, open-air walkways with hundreds of vendor stalls, plus several more enclosed buildings and open paved lots, house more than fifteen hundred vendors, who contract for their spaces on an annual basis. Except for occasional intermittent cancellations, there are no vacancies. Each space has been booked for years. This is a busy place with a carnival-like atmosphere. The market opens at 6:30 A.M. and closes at 4:00 P.M., and there's a crowd here most of the day. A sign at the entrance reads "No trespassing, except on Mondays."

They sell everything here, some of it new but most of it used. One person's discards are another's treasure—antiques, computer equipment, hunting knives, power tools, parakeets, flowers, jewelry, watches, musical instruments, golf clubs, grandfather clocks, comic books, old records, Barbie dolls (and all accessories), Matchbox cars, sports trading cards, coins, and stamps. If someone collects it, there's a vendor for it here. I see miracle kitchen appliances (World's Best Vegetable Peeler!), and at one booth I find a 1956 juke box for $1,200. There are clothes and whole bolts of fabric, bicycles and baby carriages, Nintendo games and stuffed teddy bears. No doubt you could rummage around here and find enough tools, equipment, artifacts, odds and ends, and other unclassifiable items to build a house, decorate the interior, and fill the closets with clothes and the refrigerator with food!

My favorites are the two rows of stalls filled with fresh fruits and vegetables: peaches, plums, pears, peppers, squash, nectarines, tomatoes, onions. A wonderful fresh aroma floats up and down the aisles. Speaking of food, they don't want you to go hungry while you're here, so concessionaires sell the usual assortment of corn dogs, curly fries, and Italian sausage sandwiches as well as tantalizing sweets like caramelized cinnamon-roasted pecans.

Across from the flea market on Highway 471, I drive up East Central Avenue to Webster's E. C. Rowell Public Library. E. C. Rowell's family moved to Webster in 1922. He was an Air Force pilot during World War II, and in 1965 and 1966 he was the Florida House of Representatives Speaker of the House.

Librarian Judy Lee shows me the library's Civil War Archives Museum, which has an interesting collection of artifacts, books, and old newspapers. One display case contains a Civil War–era saber, paper Confederate currency, and letters dated 1861 sent from Confederate soldiers' homes. Another case displays a Civil War–era leather ammunition case, a carpet-bag, a Confederate flag, and a cannonball. There's also a booklet that gives directions to nearby cemeteries containing Civil War graves.

Judy also helped me find books on Sumter County history. Many of the first settlers here paid for land with U. S. Government warrants issued to them for their service during the Seminole Indian Wars. Purchases with these warrants date back to the 1850s. In 1869, George Hayes opened a post office in the back of his general store. He submitted his application to the U. S. Postal Service with the community name Orange Home. The application came back rejected with a note that said there was already an Orange Home elsewhere in the state. Hayes needed a quick alternative. He glanced at the dictionary on his desk and decided to borrow the name Webster.

Webster is very proud of its agricultural heritage. On the third weekend in May, the town holds its annual Pepper Festival as a tribute to local farmers. Peppers were a major crop in this area after the turn of the century. Locals compete in a log sawing contest, a horseshoe tournament, a riding lawnmower race, and a stuffed pepper cook-off. Live entertainment and lots of good food have made the Pepper Festival a popular one since 1991.

Before heading back south, I drive up to the Dade Battlefield Historic Site, which is northwest of Webster, just east of Highway 301 on County Road 476. A monument there marks the site where Chief Micanopy, head of the Seminole Indians, led his December 1835 attack on U.S. Army soldiers under the command of Major Francis Dade. Micanopy's warriors, who outnumbered Dade's men almost three to one, ambushed and killed more than one hundred soldiers. Only three survived. Known as the Dade Massacre, this first confrontation of the Second Seminole War started when U.S. troops tried to force the Seminoles to relocate to reservations out West. The war lasted until 1842. Ultimately, many Seminoles were sent to Western reservations, but some evaded capture and fled to the swamps of the Everglades, where their descendants still live today.

DIRECTIONS: Take the Highway 50 (Brooksville) exit (Exit 301) east from I-75 to Highway 471, then head north

DON'T MISS: What else? The Sumter County Farmer's Market flea market (Remember: Mondays only)
ADDRESSES AND EVENTS: see page 202

TRILBY AND LACOOCHEE

Population: Trilby 200 (estimated); Lacoochee 1,345

JUST NORTH OF DADE CITY AND WEST of Highway 301 lies the tiny community of Trilby at the crossing of Highway 98 and County Road 575. The centerpiece of **Trilby** is the "Little Brown Church of the South," now the Trilby Methodist Church. Charter church members and Reverend T. H. Sistrunk built this wood-frame, tin-roof structure in 1897 and 1898. The building, its tall steeple rising from the covered entranceway, was relocated a short distance to its present location in 1920. Next door, a historical marker explains that the 1870s settlement of McLeod changed its name to Macon in 1885 when the first post office was opened. In 1896, the name was again changed, this time to Trilby, after George du Maurier's popular novel of the same name. Town officials also named several of the streets and the town's Svengali Square after characters from the novel.

At one time, Trilby had a bank, a school, a railway station, two hotels, a sawmill, a gristmill, a grocery store, a dry goods store, a drug-and-sundries store with a soda fountain, and a tuberculosis hospital. In the 1920s, it was a busy little town. That all changed in one afternoon in May 1925. Townspeople first spotted smoke coming from the second floor of the dry goods store around 1:00 P.M. They quickly started a bucket brigade, taking water from the water tower at the south end of town. Dade City's fire truck rushed to the scene, but during the time it took to drive the eight miles, flames had consumed all of the buildings on the west side of the railroad tracks. By 5:00 P.M., firefighters had contained the blaze, but most of downtown Trilby was gone. Some was rebuilt, but the town never fully recovered from that tragic afternoon. Thankfully, one of the buildings left standing was the Little Brown Church of the South.

Drive east on County Road 575, across Highway 301, and you'll come to another tiny community, **Lacoochee.** Like so many Florida small towns, it was the railroad that planted the seeds of this settlement when it came through in the mid-1880s. The Lacoochee Post Office was established in 1888. In 1922, the Cummer Cypress Company came to log cypress from the nearby Lacoochee Swamp and built a sawmill here. Lacoochee was a company town until the mill closed in 1959.

DIRECTIONS: Take Highway 301 north from Dade City, then take left fork at Highway 98 to go to Trilby, or turn east on CR 575 to go to Lacoochee.

DON'T MISS: The Little Brown Church of the South
ADDRESSES AND EVENTS: see page 202

DADE CITY

Population: 6,188

TWENTY-FIVE MILES NORTH OF TAMPA, the terrain begins to turn hilly as US Highway 301 rolls into Dade City, named for U.S. Army Major Francis Dade. Dade and his troops camped near here in December 1835, just days before meeting their demise at the Dade Massacre, which sparked the beginning of the Second Seminole War. (See Webster section.)

Readers of my original volumes of *Visiting Small-Town Florida* know that one of my favorite small-town pastimes is hunting for great local diners and cafés. Small towns seem to turn out the best Southern-family-recipe chefs, homemade pie and cake bakers, fish-fryers, and pit barbecuers. Some are tiny tucked-away-on-a-side-street places with simple fare, while others are right on Main Street with menus that change daily. The latter is the case with a Dade City restaurant that people come to from all over Central Florida, just to eat lunch. Dade City's most famous eatery is Lunch on Limoges on 7th Street, owned and run by Skip Mize and Phil Williams. The restaurant is adjacent to Williams Fashions, a women's boutique and gift shop. Phil is the third generation of Williamses to operate what began as Williams Department Store in 1908. Lunch on Limoges is an interesting place. Lunch tables blend right into the boutique at one end of the large room. The black-and-white checkerboard floor and tall ceilings echo the busy sounds of the open kitchen, which Skip built himself and which occupies one corner of the room. L. O. L. serves what I can best describe as Southern-gourmet fare. The chalkboard menu changes daily, and there are a few regular items. One of their best is the pecan grouper.

Dade City is an antiques and knickknack shopper's paradise, and most shops are within walking distance of the main downtown intersection of 7th Street (Highway 301) and Meridian Avenue. The Sandbar Market, Sugar Creek Antiques, Glades Pottery, Grapevine Antiques, and Church Street Antiques are just a few that are in the district. One of my favorites is The Picket Fence, which specializes in teddy bears. It's located in a bright yellow 1927 S. J. Lewis bungalow that was relocated to Meridian Avenue from 8th Street in 1995.

Each Labor Day weekend, Dade City holds its Pioneer Days Festival at the Pioneer Florida Museum on the north edge of town. When it opened in 1961, the museum displayed pioneer-era (1800s to early 1900s) farm implements and equipment that had been donated to the Pasco County Fair. Since then, the museum has expanded considerably, acquiring five pioneer-era buildings and relocating them to the museum grounds: the 1878 Enterprise Methodist Church; a shoe-repair shop built in 1913; the 1896 Trilby, Florida, train depot; a bright red one-room schoolhouse from Lacoochee, Florida, built in 1926; and an 1860s' farmhouse. Walking through the farmhouse gives me a sense of what daily life was like in the 1800s. It belonged to John Overstreet, who built it from native heart pine—cut with a steam-operated band saw and hand tools—on his eighty-acre homestead farm near here. As was customary in those days, the kitchen was in a separate building behind the house and was connected to the house by a covered walkway. If a fire started in the kitchen, it was less likely to burn down the whole house if it wasn't actually located inside the main house.

The museum's main building displays locally found pioneer artifacts plus some much older items. One display case features an impressive collection of archaic arrowheads, some dating back to 5000–3000 B.C.

Dade City is a terrific small-town escape—particularly for me when I have only half a day, since it's less than fifty minutes from my front door.

DIRECTIONS: Take Highway 301 north from Tampa. Continue north through Zephyrhills.

DON'T MISS: The Pioneer Florida Museum
ADDRESSES AND EVENTS: see page 202–203

CHRISTMAS

Population: 1,162

ON THE COUNTER AT THE POST OFFICE IN Christmas, Florida, there's a green ink pad and a box filled with rubber stamps to commemorate an assortment of holidays and special occasions. Patrons adorn their envelopes with the stamps. "Children love the stamps," post office employee Rose Harbeck tells me as she smiles from behind the counter. "They are always the most fun. When they come in to send packages to their grandparents or whomever, they always put all the stamps on them."

I ask Rose if things get hectic here right before Christmas. "Hectic? Yes, but actually it's absolutely beautiful. The only people who would come all the way to Christmas, Florida, just to mail their cards and packages are people who really love other people. Why else would they go through that much trouble just to have 'Christmas' on their postmark? So we really get to meet the finest folks. They come here from all over, many from Europe. While visiting Disney they hear about us."

Not only do people come by in person, but starting in November of each year, the Christmas post office begins receiving boxes of letters and packages to mail out with the Christmas postmark. This small post office becomes a busy clearinghouse for parcels coming in from around the world, then going back out around the world, often right back to where they came from. "We get some of our biggest boxes of letters from Germany, Italy, Spain, England, and Japan. Usually (people) include a letter to themselves as well—maybe to see if we've done a good job or not," Rose chuckles.

The Christmas postmark looks pretty much like any other: an oval with "Christmas, Florida" across the top, the date in the middle, and the 32709 zip code across the bottom. Each year, this little post office

119

stamps and mails out over three hundred thousand Christmas cards, quite a bit for an office that serves an area with a population of fewer than twelve hundred. "It starts to get crazy the day after Thanksgiving, but we love it," says Rose.

The current Christmas post office was built in 1987. Paintings on the wall depict the 1918 and 1937 post office buildings. The first post office was established in 1892 in the home of postmaster Samuel Hurlbut. His son, Van, delivered the mail twice a week on foot to as far away as Chuluota, twelve miles to the north.

Christmas was originally Fort Christmas. In only two days, United States Army troops under the command of General Abraham Eustis built the eighty-foot-by-eighty-foot log fort with two blockhouses. They began construction on December 25, 1837—hence the name. One of many forts built during the Second Seminole War (1835–1842), Fort Christmas no longer stands, but there is an impressive re-creation, built in 1977, at the Fort Christmas Historical Park on Fort Christmas Road, two miles north of State Road 50.

DIRECTIONS: Take SR 50 east from Orlando or west from Titusville.

DON'T MISS: Getting your Christmas cards stamped at the post office
ADDRESSES AND EVENTS: see page 203

YEEHAW
JUNCTION

Population: 500 (estimated)

NO BOOK ABOUT SMALL TOWNS IN FLORIDA would be complete without mentioning Yeehaw Junction. The unusual name gets everyone's attention. Some say it is a more socially acceptable version of its original name, Jackass (that's the four-legged, floppy-eared variety) Crossing. Jackasses hauled lumber to railroad loading depots in the early 1900s, and this was a major crossing on their route. Yeehaw mimics the sound a jackass makes. Others contend that the name is a variation on the Creek Indian word *yaha*, meaning "wolf."

Truck drivers and traveling salesmen in the 1940s and 1950s knew Yeehaw Junction as the intersection of two of Florida's major thoroughfares, Highway 441 and State Road 60. The Desert Inn at the intersection's northwest corner was their standard stop for fuel, food, and a night's rest. According to some, they might also find a night's illicit entertainment. George and Stephanie Zicheck bought the old inn in 1986 from the estate of Fred and Julia Cheverette, who had owned it for forty years. The Zichecks' daughter Beverly has been operating the Desert Inn since 1987.

"My parents had homes in Tampa and West Palm Beach, and Yeehaw Junction is midway between the two, so we passed by here a lot," Beverly tells me as I finish off my meat loaf sandwich and bowl of chili. "They bought the inn in nineteen eighty-six. When I first started operating it in February nineteen eighty-seven, everyone [who] came through the door would tell me, 'Please leave it like it's always been. Don't change anything.'" A 1950s Desert Inn postcard hanging on the wall is proof positive that the place does look exactly as it did back then. Even the big bougainvillea bush that grows along the west side of the inn in the postcard is still there today. A newly planted historical mark-er out front confirms that Beverly intends to keep the place as it was originally.

"When they passed the new CDL [commercial driver's license] laws, business took a dive because the truckers couldn't buy beer and liquor at the package store anymore," she explains. "I needed something to revitalize interest in the place, and that's when I decided to start work-ing on getting the Desert Inn included on the National Register of Historic Places. I can assure you that that's not something that happens easily. It was a lot of work."

During the first six months of her endeavor, she waded through Tallahassee's bureaucratic pea soup. First they sent her the wrong forms. Then they sent someone down to Yeehaw to help her, but that person was promptly transferred to another department. Finally, out of frustra-tion, Beverly called Florida State Representative Bud Bronson. Within a week she received all the correct paperwork. Then she began the task of piecing together the Desert Inn's history. Through her contacts with sev-eral historical societies, she met Lucille Wright Sturgis, a writer who had done National Register projects before. Beverly and Lucille dug through libraries and court records and interviewed people who had lived and worked in this area as far back as the 1920s. The Desert Inn was finally placed on the National Register in January 1994. The historical marker, which had just been placed two weeks prior to my visit, proclaims, "The Desert Inn was founded as a trading post in the 1880s. The present build-ing dates before 1925 and served as a supply and recreational center for the cattle drivers, lumbermen, and tourists during the era when much of Osceola County was undeveloped wilderness. . . ."

The dining room and bar end of the inn sits close to the apex of the intersection of Highways 441 and 60. The sound of air brakes and rum-bling diesels is a constant background noise. Inside, the dozen or so tables and booths are arranged around the U-shaped bar. An old Wurlitzer jukebox plays mostly country classics—George Jones, Elvis Presley. Beverly has collected some strange Florida memorabilia: plaques with clever sayings, stuffed jackalopes, rattlesnake hides, and other odd-ball knickknacks, many with a "jackass" motif. They're all hanging on the walls or displayed on shelves or on the bar. Two lifelike wooden Indians permanently occupy one corner table.

Beverly likes to play practical jokes. If you choose a corner booth, a plastic spider or bat may fall into your soup. In the ladies room (Beverly insisted that I see this) there is a life-size male mannequin. To catch the curious unaware, she has rigged a beeping alarm to the zipper on his blue jeans.

Beverly has turned the Desert Inn's upstairs rooms into a museum with railroad and lumber industry artifacts, as well as Cracker cowboy and Seminole Indian items. And then there is her "bordello" collection. Apparently in the 1940s and '50s, the upstairs portion of the inn was a popular brothel. Some of the local old-timers steadfastly deny its existence, but Beverly says she has met many previous patrons who have confirmed that it did exist. "You get some of the old cowhands in here, and they'll tell you some wild stories about this place," Beverly tells me with a grin.

You might not plan an extended four-day weekend here, but if you're passing through Yeehaw Junction, you have to stop at the Desert Inn. Visit a piece of Florida's past, have a bowl of Beverly's chili (or maybe a gator burger), and watch the eclectic mix of people that comes in— from traveling businessmen and truck drivers to cattle ranchers and cowpokes.

DIRECTIONS: At the junction of SR 60, Highway 441, and the Florida Turnpike.

DON'T MISS: The Desert Inn
ADDRESSES AND EVENTS: see page 203

ANNA MARIA
AND
HOLMES BEACH

Population: 1,844

A HUGE SHARK'S JAW HANGS ON THE WALL in the Anna Maria Island Museum. Next to it is a photo of a hammerhead caught at the Rod and Reel Pier on the north end of Anna Maria. It's the size of the great white in the movie *Jaws III*. The photo caption reads, "Record great hammerhead shark—1386 pounds, 17 feet 1 inch, 83-inch girth, 42-inch hammer. Caught by Rod and Reel Pier owner Frank Cavandish and Dr. Ralph French, 6-28-73." Fishing is certainly a popular pastime on Anna Maria, but the intense excitement of battling a record hammerhead contrasts sharply with the usual slow pace on this Gulf barrier island.

The town of **Anna Maria**, at the north end of seven-and-a-half-mile-long Anna Maria Island, has been a convenient getaway and respite for weary west coast Floridians since the early 1900s. Despite its almost ideal location south of the entrance to Tampa Bay and just offshore from Bradenton, this place has managed to fend off the usually inevitable invasion of high-rise condos and zero-lot-line dwellings and retain its quiet, beach-town flavor for more than a century.

The Anna Maria Island Historical Society runs the Anna Maria Island Museum, located in an ice house built in 1920 a few blocks east of Gulf Drive on Pine Street, the island's first road. While I visited the museum, I met and spoke to Carolyn Norwood, founder of both the historical society and the museum. In 1989, Carolyn had just left her job as a reporter for the *Islander* newspaper when Anna Maria's mayor mentioned the idea of a historical society. "He said that he thought we should have some way to preserve the island's heritage," she explained.

Anna Maria beach

"At that time, the island was not quite a hundred years old. Our centenial was in nineteen ninety-four. We had our first meeting and founded the Anna Maria Island Historical Society in November nineteen ninety. Our purpose is to collect, research, preserve, and exhibit items that pertain to Anna Maria's history. We know that, after our elder residents die, much of their belongings get thrown out, including pictures and letters. Unfortunately, some of our history gets thrown out with them. We started by running ads in the *Islander:* Please look through your attics, closets, wherever, and see if you have any old documents, artifacts, or pictures. I went to Ed Chiles, owner of the Sandbar Restaurant—he was a board member, and he's very community oriented—and I talked to him about fundraising. He said, 'I'll go out to the businesses in the community and raise money, and I'll guarantee that the museum's overhead is covered for its first year.' What he couldn't collect he paid for out of his own pocket for that entire first year. That's how we got started."

A bookcase filled with videotapes sits outside her office. "We've started interviewing Anna Maria's old-timers on video," she explains. "They tell us about things that happened here fifty, sixty, seventy years ago—usually things that aren't written down anywhere. We have about sixty tapes. We really need a room for viewing."

There are lots of maps and photos on display in the museum. A series of aerial photos shot from the 1940s through the 1990s show the changes that have taken place on the island. The biggest jump in development appears to have taken place in the 1960s. What surprises me is how much variation there has been in the shape of the island, particularly the beach on the north end called Bean Point. In some shots it juts sharply out into the Gulf; in others, it's nonexistent. In addition to the pictures and documents on display, the museum has bookshelves filled with albums of photos and news clippings. Carolyn could definitely use more wall space.

Most people assume that the name Anna Maria has a Spanish origin, and that's a reasonable assumption, since Spanish explorers, including Ponce de León and Hernando de Soto, sailed this coast in the early 1500s. Old Spanish maps that predate Florida's inclusion in the United States show the island as Ana Maria Cay. Another contingent, however, claims that the name is Scottish and should be pronounced Anna Mar-EYE-a. Many of the island's longtime residents pronounce the name with a long *i*.

George Emerson Bean stopped on uninhabited Anna Maria Island sometime in the early 1890s while sailing from his home in Connecticut down to the Gulf. He fell in love with it and vowed to return with his family. In 1893, he filed for homestead on 160 acres on the north end of the island. With the help of his sons, he built its first residence near where the Rod and Reel Pier is now. Bean died in 1898, but his sons and their families continued to live and build on Anna Maria.

John Roser was the German baker who invented the recipe for Fig Newtons. He had sold his recipe to Nabisco and moved to St. Petersburg to retire when he met George Bean Jr. In 1911, they teamed up to form the Anna Maria Beach Company and began the first commercial development of the island. That same year, the city pier was built to serve as a dock for day excursion boats from Tampa. It wasn't until 1921 that the Cortez Bridge opened, connecting Bradenton Beach at the south end of the island to the mainland. In 1913, John Roser built Anna Maria's first church as a memorial to his wife, Caroline. Each Saturday, a pastor from a different church on the mainland came to the nondenominational Roser Memorial Community Church by boat, gave services, then returned on Monday. The church is at the northeast end of Pine Avenue and is still active today.

Bungalow at the end of Oak Street

Roser Memorial Community Church on Pine Avenue

To the weekend visitor, Anna Maria is an uncrowded and unhurried beach community best traversed on a bicycle. Gulf Drive bisects the island into southeast and northwest sections. Off the beach side of Gulf Drive, a succession of two-block-long avenues with tree names like Palm, Willow, Cedar, and Maple dead-end at the beach. My favorite bungalow on the island sits at the end of Oak Street, shaded by ninety-foot-tall Australian pines right on the beach. Gulf Drive ends when it reaches Pine Avenue. This is the big intersection in Anna Maria. A block east, North Shore Drive continues up and around the north point, where the beach reaches widely out into the Gulf.

Good eateries abound on Anna Maria Island. Beach Bistro and The Sandbar (both on the beach) and Sign of the Mermaid on Gulf Drive are all exceptional make-a-reservation restaurants. My favorites, though, are the beach diners, local cafés that have a trail of beach sand leading through the front door. Anna Maria has more good ones per square mile than any town in Florida. I'll tell you about five that I recommend.

Whenever I think of Anna Maria, the first thing that pops into my mind is the Rod and Reel Pier and Café. Built in 1947 and located just around the corner from the north point on North Shore Drive, it's an island icon. The sign says, "Likely the best fishing spot in Florida. Island cooking, beer, and fun!" The two-story shack out on the end of the wooden pier has a bait-and-tackle shop downstairs and a little, short-order diner upstairs. Waves passing under the pier cause the wooden structure to sway gently back and forth. Looking northwest, diners have a view of Passage Key and Egmont Key and the Gulf beyond. To the northeast, they can see the Sunshine Skyway Bridge crossing the entrance to Tampa Bay.

The island's other pier is the Anna Maria City Pier on South Shore Drive, a little less than a mile southeast of the Rod and Reel. This one was built in 1911 and is 678 feet long. The tin-roofed buildings on the end house another bait-and-tackle shop and the City Pier Restaurant. Try the crab cakes.

"Funky" is the best way I can describe Mr. Bones BBQ on Gulf Drive, just south of Anna Maria in **Holmes Beach** (the middle section of Anna Maria Island). Bamboo wallpaper and a collection of bizarre and some downright terrifying tribal masks hang on the walls. The masks are genuine and come from around the world. Swing music playing in the background gives Mr. Bones an atmosphere associated with back-alley joints in the French Quarter of New Orleans. The menu offers ribs prepared four different ways: St. Louis style, Mongolian, Mandarin, and honey-glazed. I have the very meaty, fall-off-the-bone-tender St. Louis style, smoked and basted in a dark, sweet barbecue sauce and served with vegetable fried rice, candied yams, baked beans, and fresh-squeezed lemonade.

Ooh La La European Bistro in the Island Shopping Center serves outstanding French toast made from freshly baked baguettes, as well as unusual omelets (asparagus and onion, perhaps, or strawberry preserves?), eggs Benedict, eggs Mornay, and poached eggs on a bed of spinach, tomato, and garlic. The dinner menu is equally gourmet, with entrées like Beef Wellington and Garlic-crusted Twin Lobster Tails.

Readers of the original volume of *Visiting Small-Town Florida* will remember Duffy's, an Anna Maria beer-and-burger icon for decades. Duffy's closed in June 2002, but owner Pat Guyer has now reopened in a new location just down the road, across the street from Holmes Beach City Hall. Good news! Duffy's is one of my favorites.

If all of this sounds enticing enough to keep you here for a weekend or maybe a week, accommodations range from a few mom-and-pop motels—vintage 1950s and '60s—to cottages and houses for rent. The most luxurious accommodation is the Harrington House on Holmes Beach (see page 124). The three-story mansion made of coquina and cypress was built in 1925 and has been restored as a bed-and-breakfast. Most the second- and third-floor rooms have balconies with sweeping views of sand and Gulf. It's a gracious yet relaxed and comfortable place (as beach houses should be). Think *The Big Chill* on the beach.

Great food, great beaches, great fishing, and a disdain for intrusive commercial development combine to make Anna Maria a perfect, small Florida beach town.

DIRECTIONS: From I-75, take SR 64 (Exit 220) west to Holmes Beach. Turn north on Gulf Boulevard to Anna Maria.

DON'T MISS: The Anna Maria Island Museum and the Rod and Reel Pier

ADDRESSES AND EVENTS: see page 203–204

CORTEZ

Population: 4,491

CORTEZ MAY BE THE VERY LAST OF SOMETHING once commonplace in yesterday's Florida—a coastal commercial fishing town. It occupies the western tip of a point of land that juts out into Anna Maria Sound and can be reached from Bradenton Beach via Highway 684/Cortez Road Bridge. Almost everything in Cortez has some relationship to seafood, fishing, or boats. Signs along Cortez Road advertise smoked mullet, fresh shrimp, outboard motor repair, bait, and fishing charters. At a warehouse-size shop, Sea Hagg Nauticals, I rummage through shelves of salvaged seagoing-hardware-turned-decoration: ship's wheels, portholes, and compasses plus gold doubloons and carved driftwood art.

On the south side of Highway 684/Cortez Road, you'll find a quiet neighborhood of simple clapboard cottages. Boat docks and fish warehouses line the south shoreline of Cortez. In the mid-1800s, this peninsula was known as Hunter's Point. The locals called the area "the Kitchen" because of the abundance of seafood and shellfish that could be caught in these waters. In 1888, a post office was established here, and the name Cortez was submitted. "Cortez" may be a reference to Spanish explorer Hernando Cortes, who conquered Mexico and the Aztecs for Spain in 1519. However, there is no indication that Cortes ever explored Florida.

The town grew into a small but busy fishing community, with mullet netting, processing, and shipping the primary industry. Much of Cortez' history is divided between "before 1921" and "after 1921," when a hurricane blew in from the Gulf without warning. A storm surge destroyed the docks and sank whole fleets of fishing boats. A large passenger steamship, the *Mistletoe*, went down in the storm. Residents crowded into the town's brick schoolhouse for shelter while their

Alcee Taylor, son of Neriah Elijah Taylor, at N. E. Taylor Boatworks in Cortez

homes washed away. The only building left standing on Cortez' waterfront was the Albion Inn/Hotel.

At the south end of 23rd Street, on the south waterfront, I find a two-story structure nearly camouflaged by the palmetto scrubs, palm trees, and Australian pines that surround it. A sign over the front entranceway, hand-painted on well-weathered driftwood, reads "N. E. Taylor Boatworks." I'm debating whether or not it would be impolite to knock on the door and ask if I could take some pictures when a gentleman wearing a fishing cap walks down the outside steps. Alcee Taylor and I trade introductions. He was born in Cortez in 1923 and grew up in this house, built the same year. The upstairs was his family's home. The downstairs was his father's business, the Boatworks.

"Sometime around nineteen oh eight, my father [Neriah Elijah Taylor] moved down [from North Carolina]. His brother had come first, then he followed and brought my mother down," Alcee explains.

I've interrupted Alcee's lunch. He's snacking on a wedge of cheese but doesn't seem to mind the intrusion and leads me in through the side door. "The foundation of this house and the siding was built from driftwood lumber that washed away from down at Longboat Pass during the storm

*N. E. Taylor Boatworks in Cortez, where Neriah Elijah Taylor began
his boat building business around 1908*

of nineteen twenty-one. My father built boats in here. I've been taking all the old tools and equipment and kind of making it into a museum."

Inside, seventy-five years' worth of woodworking and boat-building equipment—every size and shape of saw, all variety of hand drills, jigs, and templates—fills what was once a small factory for building eighteen- to twenty-foot pole skiffs and twenty-two- to twenty-six-foot V-hull launches. Back then, two iron rails, used for sliding completed boats down to the water, ran the length of the floor, out the back overhead door, and into the bay.

"In the middle there is where the cradle came up to pull boats out," Alcee explains as we carefully weave our way through his father's shop, around stacks of wood and materials used decades ago for constructing boats. He points out items of interest as we pass them. "There's one of the patterns used for building a skiff. And this here is a natural-crook cedar timber." He holds up a hefty tree limb that has grown into an arc. "You had to go out into the mangrove swamps, off Longboat Key, to find pieces of wood with just the right bend in them to make your framing for the boat. They had to all line up, where you could carry the flare back on each side of the boat. You'd saw them down the center with the cross-cut saw and have two matching pieces, one for each side of the keel."

Alcee's two older brothers built boats with his father. Alcee didn't build them himself, but he did help haul lumber back from the woods. "There were a lot more mosquitoes back then," he recalls. "I've seen them so thick on the screen window upstairs that you had to beat the screen to get air to flow through."

In addition to displaying all of N. E. Taylor's boat-building equipment, Alcee has compiled a large collection of old photographs and newspaper articles. He shows me before- and after-1921 hurricane photos of the docks in Cortez. Then he pulls out a 1932 N. E. Taylor Boatworks invoice for a completed boat. It reads, "Boat: $350.00. Lumber: $65.00." They charged two dollars for a "pull-out" to winch the boat out of the water. He pulls out a receipt from Southern Utilities Company, dated June, 12, 1925. "That's when we got electricity and lights put in the house."

The centerpiece of Alcee's museum is a 1936 donkey boat. Why is it called a donkey boat? "Back in them days they used tractors, Model-Ts, horses, mules, donkeys, whatever, to pull the nets in from the beaches. My dad had bought a motor that he was going to put over there with the winch so he'd have power to pull up [boats] with. Some fishermen got to talking with him. They figured they could mount that motor in a boat, hook it to a truck transmission and a pulley, anchor the boat out in the water, run a rope out, and pull nets with it. That's what they did. It took the place of the donkey, so they called it a donkey boat."

I ask Alcee if he's seen a lot of changes in Cortez over the years. "Yeah," he says, then hesitates a moment. "Too many. And not for the good." In 1995, a referendum-voted net ban went into effect. No nets larger than five hundred square feet could be used. It was the most hotly debated item on Florida's November 1994 ballot. It pitted sport fishermen, who claimed that commercial netters were depleting the fish population, against commercial fishermen. The pro–net ban group waged ad campaigns that showed dolphins and turtles snagged in the nets of large, offshore netting trawlers. Ironically, these particular operations work far enough offshore to be outside the state's jurisdiction and are therefore not subject to the ban. The smaller, closer-to-shore commercial fishermen were legislated into immediate near-extinction. Obviously, Cortez was and is vehemently anti–net ban. Signs in front yards and on bumper stickers proclaimed it. Alcee comments, "I appreciate all them people who afterwards told me they was misled. And they was. We didn't have the money to put out what we had to say, on the TV and in the magazines and all, like they [the pro–net ban group] did. Yeah, the voters was misled. And communities like Cortez and whole generations of families whose lives have centered around fishing will pay the price."

On living here, Alcee tells me, "I do like Cortez. There are good folks here. You can still get out and walk around whenever and wherever you want to."

On my way out of Cortez I stop at Annie's Bait and Tackle, next to the bridge, for a quick bite. A sign above the bar lauds their smoked mullet spread. "Sorry. We're out," the waitress says. "Can't get mullet regularly like we used to." I settle for the barbecued pork sandwich and am subtly reminded that things in Cortez may never again be like they used to be.

DIRECTIONS: Go east of Bradenton Beach across the Highway 684 Bridge, or west of I-75 off Exit 220 (SR 64), which leads to Highway 684/Cortez Road.

DON'T MISS: N. E. Taylor Boatworks Museum
ADDRESSES AND EVENTS: see page 204

LAKE PLACID

Population: 1,668

HIGHWAY 27 CARVES ITS WAY THROUGH the Highlands County hills south of Sebring. From the road you can see for miles in any direction. Elevated vistas like these are not common in this region of Florida. Broad, rolling hills alternate with lakes in the low spots. Like a very small mountain range, the Lake Wales Ridge runs parallel to Highway 27 about twelve miles to the east. I think I know why Melvil Dewey fell in love with this area the first time he saw it.

It was in 1927 that seventy-six-year-old Dr. Melvil Dewey—the same Dewey who invented the Dewey decimal library cataloging system—came to Florida in search of a southern version of his hometown, Lake Placid, New York. What Dewey envisioned was a resort that would mirror the Lake Placid Club but with a milder climate in winter. He knew he had found what he was looking for when he first laid eyes on the small agricultural community of Lake Stearns. Dewey wasted no time in making arrangements with local landowners. In 1928, Lake Stearns incorporated under its new name, Lake Placid. Names of two of the surrounding lakes were also changed: Lake Childs became Lake Placid, and Lake Stearns became Lake June-in-Winter (The New York lake is simply Lake June.) Sadly, Dewey wasn't able to enjoy his new-found paradise for very long. Although Florida provided a welcome respite from his chronic bronchitis, Melvil Dewey passed away three short years after moving here. But with plans already under way, his widow, Emily, continued to develop his dream. The Great Depression stunted progress in the early and mid-1930s, but ultimately Lake Placid grew into the attractive community that it is today. It is still growing, not so much in size but in character.

Looming over the horizon is the 270-foot-high Placid Tower. When it was built in 1960, it was the tallest concrete masonry structure in the world. Nearly five thousand tons of concrete and steel reinforcing beams went into its construction. The $3 admission fee for the elevator ride to the top is more than worth it. There, the open-air Eagle's Nest is 360 feet above sea level, and it's the perfect place to begin a visit to Lake Placid.

From the west side, you overlook downtown Lake Placid, actually called uptown by locals. The city limits extend only around the uptown area, which technically makes the city of Lake Placid only one and a quarter miles square. Lakes border it on two sides. Lake June-in-Winter wraps around the west side of uptown, with several smaller lakes to the south. Further to the south, you can see Lake Placid. Citrus groves cover much of the hilly countryside.

The view from the east side offers something special in late August and September: acres and acres of fields filled with brightly colored caladium plants. Lake Placid is the Caladium Capital of the World. Ninety-five percent of the caladiums sold commercially around the world are grown right here in Highlands County. You can see the different varieties grown in large strips and squares. From the top of the Placid Tower, the fields look like a giant patchwork quilt of bright red, pink, white and green. A temperate climate and an abundance of boggy muck-soil near the lakes make this area ideal for growing caladiums, though they're not native to Florida. Caladiums originated in the Amazon basin and were brought to the United States for the Chicago World's Fair in 1893. They were first grown commercially in Apopka in the 1920s. Occasional winter freezing temperatures forced the industry to move further south in the 1930s, eventually finding the perfect home in Lake Placid and Highlands County. Beyond the caladium fields is twenty-seven-thousand-acre Lake Istokpoga, the largest in the county. Famous for record largemouth bass, it's the angler's favorite.

From the Placid Tower it is only a one-block stroll to the Winn Dixie grocery store. Ordinarily, I wouldn't put a grocery store on my list of things to see, but this one is different. On its outside south wall is a mural of epic proportions. At 35 feet high and 175 feet long, it's a panoramic depiction called *Cracker Trail Cattle Drive*. Artist Keith Goodson has painted a hauntingly realistic scene that shows Florida "Cracker" cowboys of yester-

Cracker Trail Cattle Drive mural, Keith Goodson

year moving their herds across the southern plains of the state. The term Cracker comes from the cracking of the whips used to maneuver the herds of cattle, and it stuck as a nickname for Florida cowboys. Some of the cows almost seem to follow my movement as I walk from one end of the mural to the other. Listen carefully and you'll hear the cracking whips and moo-ing cows of a Florida cattle drive. The Lake Placid Mural Society calls it "moosic"—it's piped through speakers on the roof to add another dimen-sion to the mural experience.

There are currently thirty-four murals throughout Lake Placid and two more in the works. Most are downtown or within walking distance. Each portrays people, places, history, or wildlife of local significance. The Lake Placid Mural Society reviews renderings submitted by artists from around the state, then handles all the subsequent arrangements once a project is agreed on. It is a testament to the enthusiasm of this community that sponsorship of and funding for the murals come solely from local businesses, service organizations, fund drives, and individuals. No tax dollars are spent.

One of my favorite murals is *Prairie Dwellers* by artist Guy LaBree at

Terry Smith's The Last Bear Cub mural

John Gutcher's Lake Placid Drug Store mural

Interlake Boulevard and Magnolia Street. It's thirty-eight feet long and eight feet high and shows a south Florida prairie with some native residents: gopher turtle, burrowing owls, deer, turkey, and wild hogs. Study it carefully and you might find a one-inch-tall Seminole Indian spirit man. Another mural with its own soundtrack is *The Lost Bear Cub*, which faces John's Park on Interlake Boulevard. Bears growl and bees buzz in this creation by Terry Smith on the side of Tony's Barber Shop. Across the street, you'll do a double take when you see John Gutcher's *Lake Placid Drug Store*, which is painted on the front of the actual Lake Placid Drug Store. It depicts the view through the front window as it appeared more than fifty years ago. Six of Lake Placid's murals are Gutcher's. The best way to see all of the murals and to read about the artists is to pick up a copy of *The Murals of Lake Placid* at the chamber of commerce on Oak Street.

You can also get a copy of the booklet at the Caladium Arts and Crafts Co-op on Interlake Boulevard. The co-op is a ten-thousand-square-foot store, gallery, and showcase for the work of its more than two hundred members, all Highlands County artists and craftspeople. They also hold seminars, workshops, and art classes. The co-op is filled with paintings, sketches, wall hangings, pottery, wood carvings, dolls, and other locally crafted artifacts.

With its murals and the efforts of the Caladium Arts and Crafts Co-op, Lake Placid is gaining a much-deserved reputation as an arts community. The resulting revitalization is evident up and down Interlake Boulevard and Main Street, where antiques shops, bookstores, restaurants, and other new businesses are popping up regularly. What is most impressive is that the chamber of commerce, local businesses, and individuals in the community have formed an enthusiastic and cohesive team to make these changes happen.

DIRECTIONS: Sixteen miles south of Sebring on Highway 27

DON'T MISS: The murals and Placid Tower
ADDRESSES AND EVENTS: see page 204–205

ARCADIA

Population: 6,604

WHEN I THINK OF ARCADIA, THREE THINGS immediately come to mind: the beautiful and appropriately named Peace River, which flows right by Arcadia on its way to Charlotte Harbor; antiques; and the fresh-baked pies at Wheeler's Goody Café. It was a sad day for me when I discovered in 2000 that Wheeler's Goody Café had closed its doors after seventy years. Diner connoisseur Mark Hammond introduced me to Wheeler's twenty years ago. It became a standard stop for me whenever I passed through Arcadia. It was the oldest continuously operated restaurant in DeSoto County. A block south of Oak Street on Monroe, Wheeler's looked like a hole in the wall, but locals knew it had the best Southern, home-cooked grub within a hundred miles, not to mention the best homemade pies on the planet.

Wheeler's began as Fiegel's Goody Café in 1929, when fifty cents would buy a good, hot lunch. Alene Davis was a waitress at Fiegel's in the 1930s. She married the owner, C. B. Fiegel, and they ran the café together until he died in 1951. When Alene was remarried to Walter Wheeler, she changed the name to Wheeler's Goody Café. After she passed away in 1994, Eddie and June Tang took it over until it closed in 2000. But, on a visit in November 2002, I peeked through Wheeler's dusty windows to find Chuck and Martha Craven in the process of remodeling the café's interior. Chuck and Martha moved to Punta Gorda from Charleston, South Carolina, where they had operated a bed-and-breakfast. And now they were reviving Wheeler's Goody Café.

"We located two of the ladies who originally baked pies for Wheeler's—peanut butter, butterscotch, coconut cream, and (my

West Oak Street

favorite) vanilla peanut butter," Chuck told me. "Our plan is to restore as much of the original Wheeler's as possible, including Mrs. Wheeler's recipes. We'll have the lunch counter and booths just like the original, and we'll be open for breakfast and lunch six days a week." I passed through Arcadia again in February 2003. Chuck and Martha had just reopened Wheeler's the month before. The place looked great, and that vanilla peanut butter pie was just as heavenly as I remember.

Visitors to Arcadia might note that a disproportionate number of buildings downtown say "Built in 1906" on them. On Thanksgiving night in 1905, Arcadia suffered the most devastating disaster in its history. A fire—the cause of which has never been determined—began in a downtown livery stable. High winds rapidly spread the flames. The townspeople fought valiantly to extinguish it, but at that time Arcadia had no public water system or firefighting equipment. By dawn, all of downtown except for three brick buildings had been consumed. Miraculously, no one died.

Two days later, Arcadia's business leaders passed the city's first building codes, which stated that all reconstruction had to be done with brick

Wheeler's Goody Cafe

or concrete. Not long after, they built a city water supply and organized a fire department. Arcadia rose, like the proverbial phoenix from the ashes, to become a thriving south central Florida community.

Lately, Arcadia has become a popular antiques shopping locale. In four blocks along Oak Street (the town's main street), I count nineteen antiques shops plus the Heard Opera House Museum, which also has antiques booths. The Mediterranean-style Opera House, built in 1906, occupies an entire city block at the corner of Oak Street and Polk Avenue in the center of downtown. In the 1910s, Arcadians strolled up these steps on Saturday evenings to watch plays and traveling vaudeville shows. When silent movies emerged in the 1920s, this became the movie theater.

Now the stage and dressing rooms have been converted into a museum. A 1902 Deere and Webbe (forerunner of the John Deere Company) horse buggy and an Indian dugout canoe of undetermined age (brought up from the bottom of the Peace River) dominate the stage. Props, costumes, handbills, and newspaper clippings from early

Arcadia Opera House days hang on the walls. The signatures of performers along with the names of their performances are still visible where they were scrawled on the dressing room walls, as was the custom with traveling shows in the 1900s and 1910s. Old movie projectors, film reels, theater seats, and silent-movie equipment preserved from the 1920s and 1930s are also on display.

Arcadia is as close to Mayberry as Floridians can get. The charming Arcadia Drug Store has been at the corner of Oak and Monroe Streets since 1916. Lucy's Southern Hair, at the other end of Oak Street, resembles a 1950s beauty parlor. Speaking of the 1950s, Brenda Lee's Deli Café (a block from Lucy's) is decorated with memorabilia from that era. And the Arcadia Tea Room (on Oak Street) and the Hot Fudge Shop (around the corner on Polk Street) are, like Arcadia itself, reminders of a bygone time.

DIRECTIONS: Located at the junction of Highway 17 and SR 70, 25 miles northeast of Port Charlotte and 50 miles southeast of Bradenton.

DON'T MISS: Wheeler's Goody Café
ADDRESSES AND EVENTS: see page 205–206

SOUTH REGION

Stuart

INDIAN
RIVER

CHARLOTTE   GLADES

BOCA
GRANDE

LA BELLE

BOKEELIA

CLEWISTON

LEE

PINELAND
MATLACHA

Fort Myers

Palm
Beach

PALM BEACH

ST. JAMES CITY

ESTERO

HENDRY

CAPTIVA
SANIBEL

Naples

BROWARD

COLLIER

75

OCHOPEE

Fort
Lauderdale

EVERGLADES
CITY

CHOKOLOSKEE

DADE

MONROE

Miami

N

1

TAVERNIER

NO NAME KEY

ISLAMORADA

Key West

1

BIG PINE KEY

BOCA GRANDE

Population: 975

RUTHLESS PIRATE AND NOTORIOUS WOMANIZER José Gaspar had decided it was time to hang up his cutlass and retire on his plunder—in other words, quit while he was ahead. It was 1821, and Florida, no longer belonging to his mother country, Spain, had just become an American state. One winter evening, Gaspar's watchmen spotted a ship—by all appearances, a British merchant vessel—chugging south. Probably on its way back from New Orleans, Gaspar thought. It would be such easy pickings for him and his crew. Maybe one final hurrah was in order. They boarded his corsair, the *Gasparilla II*, and sailed out from Gasparilla Island to intercept the ship. As they pulled alongside, it lowered the Union Jack and raised the Stars and Stripes! Then camouflage was dropped off the deck, revealing a battery of cannons. Gaspar had been duped. It was a trick worthy of his own design. He and his men were no match for this United States man-of-war, the USS *Enterprise*. Its cannons pounded the *Gasparilla II*, intent on reducing it to kindling. In the heat of battle, Gaspar marched to the bow, wrapped the anchor chain around his waist, and stepped off the edge, cursing his attackers as he tumbled into the brine.

The story of José Gaspar was told repeatedly by a crusty old Cuban fisherman, Juan Gomez, also known as Panther Key John. Actually, "old" is an understatement. Reputedly, Juan Gomez was 119 years old when he died in 1900. It seems that a bottle of rum was all that was required to get him started telling tales about Gaspar, whom Gomez claimed had employed him for most of his first forty years. Those who would listen said that the stories varied some, depending on the volume of rum

Gomez consumed, but Gaspar was always portrayed as ferocious, flamboyant, and feared by all.

Over the decades, several variations on Gaspar's entrance into piratehood have been recited. One version tells that José Gaspar was a young lieutenant in the Spanish Royal Navy in 1783. Spain was at war with the British, who had amassed a powerful navy. The Spanish Navy was in a retreat-and-repair mode, leaving some of their ships idle at sea. Out of frustration with their inactivity, Gaspar convinced his fellow crewmen onboard the *Florida Blanca* to mutiny. They murdered their captain and his few supporters and sailed for Florida. Gaspar pulled down the Spanish flag, raised the skull and crossbones, renamed the 110-foot fighting vessel the *Gasparilla*, and changed his own name to Gasparilla.

Another version has Spanish Navy "Admiral" José Gaspar falsely accused of stealing some of the royal jewels from King Charles III. To save his neck, he stole one of the Navy's ships with the help of a small band of criminals. They sailed off for the Caribbean and never looked back. He and his crew adopted Gasparilla Island as their headquarters. It was the ideal location for launching attacks on merchant ships traveling between Cuba and New Orleans. They built High Town, their version of Jamaica's Port Royal.

Gaspar was said to be an incorrigible ladies' man. The most consistently told tale about him concerns his capturing a Spanish vessel forty miles off Boca Grande in 1801. His crew murdered all onboard except eleven Mexican girls and one Spanish princess, Josefa. The eleven were sent to nearby Captiva Island, but Gaspar kept Josefa for himself. He fell madly in love with the princess. He showered her with gifts and treated her with as much royalty as he could muster, but she would have nothing to do with him. Confounded by her loathing of him, Gaspar chopped off her head in a fit of rage. The murder reportedly took place on Josefa Island (now called Useppa Island), south of Boca Grande between Cayo Costa and Pine Island. The headless ghost of Josefa is said to roam both Useppa and Gasparilla Islands to this day.

The existence of José Gaspar has been a matter of dispute for nearly one hundred years. In 1936, *Tampa Morning Tribune* editor Edwin Lambright wrote *The Life and Exploits of Gasparilla, Last of the Buccaneers*. In it he claims that Spanish Navy records and ships' logs and Gaspar's own diary, confiscated by the Spanish government, offer documented proof that he was real. The *Pirates Who's Who* by Philip Gosse, published in 1924, refers to him as factual. More recent searches, however, lean toward his being a fictional character. It's likely that Gasparilla Island was really named after a group of Spanish priests who ran a mission in Charlotte Harbor. Old charts, predating Gaspar's presumed lifetime, show Gasparilla Pass as Friar Gaspar Pass. Now most historians concur: Gaspar was nothing more than the polluted figment of Juan Gomez's imagination.

In 1918, the Charlotte Harbor and Northern Railroad released a publication, *The Gasparilla Story*, which pieced together some of Gomez's anecdotes. This publication, which most current historians think spread the story's popularity, also contained sales advertisements for railroad-owned property in Boca Grande, the terminus of the railway on Gasparilla Island. The sales efforts turned out to be lackluster, but the romanticized story of José Gaspar became accepted as fact. There is little doubt that real pirates did frequent this coast and probably visited Gasparilla Island in the 1700s. Pirate Henri Caesar, known as Black Caesar, made Sanibel Island his headquarters in the late 1700s.

For most of the 1800s, Gasparilla Island's few inhabitants were transient—some Cuban mullet fishermen and maybe a few rumrunners. In 1885, phosphate was discovered mid-state and was being transported down the Peace River and out to Charlotte Harbor. Suddenly, Gasparilla Island, at the mouth of Charlotte Harbor, was an important piece of property. The town of Boca Grande (Spanish for "big mouth," referring to Boca Grande Pass at the mouth of Charlotte Harbor) sprung up at the island's southern end to accommodate workers unloading phosphate from river barges and reloading it onto ships sailing abroad. In 1907, the Charlotte Harbor and Northern Railroad replaced the river barges.

For the better part of a century, generations of Florida families have been coming to Boca Grande for its relaxed island atmosphere and its world-famous tarpon fishing. Gasparilla Island is accessible only by the $3.50 toll bridge at its north end or by boat. The island's relative isolation has allowed it to develop a unique personality. It's almost always unhurried and uncrowded. There are no stoplights, and the only structure more than three stories tall is the steel-girder lighthouse next to the public beach. There is some wildlife here—a variety of seabirds and plenty of raccoons. A few decades ago, someone let a pair of pet iguanas loose. Now, spotting some of their descendents sunning on a seawall is common.

Boca Grande is big on fishing tournaments. Many of them are during tarpon season, mid-April through mid-July. The biggest one, the World's

Richest Tarpon Tournament (catch-and-release), takes place the second weekend in July and is sponsored by the Boca Grande Area Chamber of Commerce. First place is $250,000.

You can easily spot the "tournies." They all wear oversize, vented cotton shirts and long-billed caps with a built-in flap that covers the neck, like the one John Wayne wore in *Hatari*. Boca Grande is the undisputed tarpon fishing capital of the world. The tarpon is king here. Tarpon are actually called silver kings because their giant scales reflect like mirrors. Every restaurant, grocery store, boutique, and office has a stuffed tarpon (or facsimile thereof) hanging on the wall. Sometimes weighing more than two hundred pounds, this big, prehistoric-looking fish is inedible, so all tarpon fishing is catch-and-release. In the tournaments, they are weighed, measured, and photographed at the boat, then released. Today, taxidermists recreate the stuffed versions completely from fiberglass using photos and measurements.

Besides fishing, visitors to Boca Grande can swim, sail, walk the beach, get an ice cream cone at the old train depot, or browse the shops in the quaint four blocks of downtown. My favorite shop is Fugate's. Opened in 1916, it is the oldest continuous business on the island and is still run by the Fugate family. It reminds me of a beach five-and-dime that I recall from my childhood summer vacations in the 1960s. Jerome Fugate Sr. was hired to manage the Boca Grande Mercantile Company General Store in 1911. Five years later, he sold his minority interest in it and bought a small local drug store and soda fountain. Fugate's became the town's most popular gathering place, and it's still a hub of activity today.

The primary mode of transportation in Boca Grande is the electric golf cart. Everybody has one. There's even a golf cart path that runs the length of the north end of the island into town. Island Bike 'N Beach rents golf carts and bicycles (see appendix).

The island boasts some excellent restaurants. Among my favorites is Temptations on Park Avenue (Boca Grande's main street), which specializes in fresh local seafood. Dining there is like traveling in a time machine back to the 1940s. The décor in Temptations has remained largely unchanged since it opened in 1947. The bar is *the* place to hear big-fish stories. Across the street, in the old San Marcos Theater Building (a movie house when it was built in the late 1920s), you'll find PJ's Seagrille. The salad dressings and soups are made fresh in-house daily. Try the tomato basil bisque with lump blue crab. Loons on a Limb, at

Third Street and East Railroad, is the best breakfast spot. You might have to wait briefly for a table, but it will be worth it. For pastries and coffee, try Boca Grande Baking Company on East Railroad. I like their giant, fresh-baked doughnuts.

Many of Boca Grande's earliest buildings are still in use. The two oldest churches on the island, the United Methodist at Third Street and Gilchrist Avenue and the First Baptist at Fourth Street and Gilchrist, were built in 1910 and 1915, respectively. Back then, they would alternate Sunday services to ensure good attendance. The Gilchrist Avenue area, which covers several blocks south of downtown, was purchased and developed in the 1890s by Albert Gilchrist, who would become Florida's twentieth governor. Many of the restored homes there date back to that era.

Banyan trees line both sides of Banyan Street, a block south of Third Street. Bostonian Peter Bradley, founder of the American Agricultural Chemical Company, planted them in 1914. A banyan tree's roots grow out of its limbs and down to the ground, giving it an unusual, sometimes ghostly, appearance. The trees on Banyan Street have grown to form a tunnel-like canopy over the street.

Further south are Boca Grande's two lighthouses. The first one, a 105-foot-tall, steel-girder structure, stands next to the public beach and has the year 1927 stamped on its door. The second one, at the southern tip of the island, serves as a channel marker for Boca Grande Pass. Built in 1890, it is thought to be the oldest building on Gasparilla Island. It fell into disrepair in the 1960s, but it was donated to the county in 1972 and added to the National Register of Historic Places in 1980. The Department of Natural Resources took over ownership in 1985. The wooden lighthouse was restored, a new light was installed, and it was recommissioned in 1986. Boca Grande Lighthouse and its matching assistant keeper's house next door can be toured on the last Saturday of each month from 10 A.M. to 4 P.M.

Boca Grande's most regal edifice is the Gasparilla Inn. It was built in 1911 as the Hotel Boca Grande, a simple, twenty-room hotel. By 1913, it had been expanded and its name changed to Gasparilla Inn. In 1930, industrialist Barron G. Collier bought it and added a solarium and columns to the front entrance. Today, it's an opulent resort in the tradition of Collier's era with a golf course, tennis courts, swimming pools, full-service spa, and an array of other amenities. The main hotel has 154 rooms. Nineteen additional quadruplex cottages (which can be opened

Boca Grande Lighthouse

up to accommodate families or groups) occupy several blocks in the surrounding neighborhood. Citrus trees, Australian pines, and towering palms grow throughout the grounds. The cottages are open year-round, but the main inn is open only from mid-December through mid-June. The inn's owner for the past three decades, Bayard Sharp, passed away in 2002. Grandson Bill Farish has taken over its operation.

As island regulars will tell you, Boca Grande is the grandest.

DIRECTIONS: From I-75, take Highway 777/Englewood exit (Exit 191). Follow Highway 777 southwest through Englewood to Highway 775. Go south on Highway 775 to Gasparilla Island and Boca Grande.

DON'T MISS: The Temptation Restaurant and Fugate's
ADDRESSES AND EVENTS: see page 206–207

LA BELLE AND CLEWISTON

Population: La Belle 4,210; Clewiston 6,460

SISTERS FLORA AND ELLA BURCHARD (who married two brothers) opened their restaurant specializing in Southern-style home cooking in the small agricultural town of **La Belle** in 1933. They served hearty, country meals to a hardworking community with a big appetite. Roast turkey and dressing, fried chicken, black-eyed peas, fried okra, sweet corn, pickled beets, and mashed potatoes and gravy are just some of the Southern staples they served, but their specialty was (and still is) pies. For decades, towering coconut, peanut butter, and chocolate meringues; pecan pies; and a variety of fruit pies are what have kept a steady flow of customers lined up, waiting for a table. Even the sign out front acknowledges it: "Flora and Ella's, Since 1933, Home of Those Famous Pies."

Ella passed away in 1998, Flora in 2002. A few years back they had decided to take it a little easier and let Ella's daughter Irene and her husband, Alan Trask, take over running the place. So folks wouldn't have to wait as long for a table, Alan and Irene relocated the restaurant to a new, larger building around the corner and down the road from the original, which was on Bridge Street by the Caloosahatchee River.

The first time I visited Flora and Ella's, Debbie Burchard (Irene's daughter, Ella's granddaughter) waited on me. That time I had the fried catfish (Alan's specialty) with grits, light crispy-fried hush puppies, coleslaw, and collard greens. Along with my meal, Debbie brought me one of those plastic squeeze bottles of honey shaped like a bear.

"Squirt some honey on those hush puppies," she told me with a smile. "It's really good, and I brought you some cornbread to dip in the pot liquor." That's the juice from the collard greens. "And make sure you save room for pie."

"What's the most popular pie?" I asked Debbie.

"Coconut cream," she told me. "But, I have to warn you, it's just come out of the oven, so it'll probably still be warm. I tell people that now because, the other day, I had a lady who complained because she wanted hers cold."

Oh, no! Not warm, fresh-out-of-the-oven pie! She brought back a fat wedge of the coconut cream pie, with its gravity-defying meringue peaking to five inches at the point. It looked like the bow of the *Titanic*. It was still warm, and it was melt-in-your-mouth delicious.

On my most recent visit, I found that Debbie has now taken over running the restaurant, which is as busy as ever. This time I ordered the Country Boy pot roast, which was so tender it pulled apart with a fork. I had mashed potatoes and turnip greens on the side. The roast and potatoes were smothered in a delicious, rich, brown gravy. For dessert I opted for the peanut butter cream pie, which was wonderful. The choice was not an easy one, though. I could have had pecan, coconut cream, apple, chocolate cream, key lime, lemon meringue, or pumpkin, all baked fresh that morning.

Continue east on State Road 80 and you'll reach **Clewiston**, a town on the south bank of Lake Okeechobee. This is sugarcane country. United States Sugar Corporation, the country's largest and oldest sugarcane producer, has had its headquarters in Clewiston since the 1920s, when it was the Southern Sugar Company. U.S. Sugar farms on 175,000 acres in three counties that border Lake Okeechobee's south side.

The noble Clewiston Inn, the oldest hotel on Lake Okeechobee, is in the center of town at the corner of Sugarland Highway (Highway 27) and Royal Palm Avenue. It fronts a city park, on the far side of which are the corporate offices of the United States Sugar Corporation. Originally built in 1926, the inn was destroyed by a fire in 1937. U.S. Sugar rebuilt the inn in 1938 to accommodate and entertain visiting executives and dignitaries. Four two-story white columns support a traditional Southern gable that protrudes over the inn's entrance. Neatly pruned palm trees line the circular drive where it swings underneath the gable. This is a Rhett-and-Scarlett kind of place. Bird's-eye cypress paneling covers the lobby walls all the way up to its open-beam ceiling. The terra cotta tile floor is waxed to a glossy shine. A wide staircase with brass railings leads to the second floor. The rooms are comfortable and decorated in a simple yet elegant 1940s style. When you check in, you'll receive a bag of sugar cookies. This is, after all, the "Sweetest Town in America."

Clewiston Inn

*Part of the J. Clinton Shepherd mural that wraps around all four walls
in the Clewiston Inn's Everglades Lounge*

I came to the inn because I had heard about the J. Clinton Shepherd oil-on-canvas mural that wraps around all four walls in the inn's Everglades Lounge. Shepherd lived at the inn for the better part of 1945. Every day he took treks into the Everglades to sketch Florida's native wild animals and plants. When he felt that he had accumulated enough material, he began to put his subjects on canvas. The result is a hauntingly beautiful and remarkably real 360-degree panorama, set in an early morning mist and depicting most of the wildlife that calls the Everglades home. Every variety of native duck, egret, heron, and crane can be found somewhere on these walls. Owls, jays, and ospreys also make an appearance, as do deer, opossums, a marsh hare, raccoons, alligators, and a black bear with her cub. The mural is one continuous scene. Shepherd had to precisely measure and cut the canvas to fit around windows, cabinets, and the doorway. You almost feel as though you're standing in the middle of a cypress bay head at daybreak.

The inn has been at the center of life in Clewiston throughout the town's history. During World War II, the British Royal Air Force trained cadets at nearby Riddle Field. The Clewiston Inn was the flyboys' favorite hangout. The inn's caretakers have done an excellent job of adhering to the ambiance of that grand era.

This area's biggest attraction is what the Seminole Indians called the "Big Water." More than 730 square miles in area and 35 miles in diameter, Lake Okeechobee is a virtual inland sea. It is the second largest freshwater lake wholly within the United States' boundaries. To avid anglers, it is Nirvana. They come here for largemouth bass, bluegill, speckled perch, and Okeechobee catfish. If you're here to fish, don't miss stopping in at Roland Martin's Marina, Motel, Resort, Café, RV Park, Ship's Store and Guide Service. Arguably the most famous bass fisherman in the world, Martin is a regular top-finisher in the biggest bass tournaments, and he also has his own cable TV fishing show. His shop in Clewiston sells every imaginable piece of fishing paraphernalia, clothes, and lake charts. If it has anything to do with fishing, it's in here.

On September 16, 1928, tragedy struck Lake Okeechobee when a hurricane with 160-mile-per-hour winds crossed the lake from the Atlantic Ocean. The hurricane's front winds pushed the water in Lake Okeechobee to the north, flooding the town of Okeechobee. As it passed over, moving west, the winds from the backside of the hurricane pushed the water back south and flooded Pahokee, Belle Glade, and

Clewiston. More than two thousand people drowned. Rescuers continued to find bodies weeks after the storm. Many of them were Bahamian migrant workers, and there was no way to identify them. In response to the disaster, in the early 1930s, the U.S. Army Corps of Engineers built 140 miles of forty-foot-high levees around the lake, which you will see if you are driving east out of Clewiston.

DIRECTIONS: From I-75, take the SR 80 exit (Exit 141) east to La Belle. Continue east on SR 80 to Highway 27 and go east to Clewiston.

DON'T MISS: Flora and Ella's Restaurant in La Belle and J. Clinton Shepherd's wildlife mural in the Clewiston Inn's Everglades Lounge

ADDRESSES AND EVENTS: see page 207

MATLACHA, BOKEELIA, ST. JAMES CITY, AND PINELAND

Population: Matlacha 735;
Bokeelia 1,997; St. James City 4,105; Pineland 444

SOUTHWEST FLORIDA'S GULF COAST IS ONE of the state's fastest growing regions, but this is still a great place to find tropical isolation. Some of the Pine Island Sound communities, such as Useppa and North Captiva, can be reached only by boat. Tiny, hundred-acre Cabbage Key, home to

The Waterfront Restaurant, St. James City

the Cabbage Key Inn and Restaurant, is a perennial favorite for boaters looking for a great cheeseburger for lunch. Those towns you can drive to—the communities of Pine Island—range from sleepy Old Florida to tropical paradise.

State Road 78 rolls west through North Fort Myers and eventually becomes the only bridge that connects Pine Island to the mainland. The first stop on the island side of the bridge is **Matlacha**, pronounced Mat-la-*shay* with a French flair, although there's nothing French about it. Matlacha encompasses the smaller, stepping-stone islands that State Road 78 hops across just before it takes you onto Pine Island. Fishing boats bob up and down at their moorings behind the restaurants and gift shops that line both sides of the highway. Fishing, fishing boats, fishing tackle, eating fish, fish art—everything revolves around fish in Matlacha. The State Road 78 bridge is referred to as the "fishingest bridge in the world." Once a year, locals even hold a mullet-throwing contest here!

Pine Island is Florida's largest Gulf Coast island. It's seventeen miles long and three miles wide. State Road 78 intersects Stringfellow Road, the island's main thoroughfare, which connects St. James City at its southern tip with Bokeelia at its northern tip. The straight, two-lane road passes through groves and past nurseries. Pine Island has a thriving, subtropical, exotic fruit and plant industry. Best known for its mangoes, which early settlers began growing here at the turn of the century, the island also supports pineapple, carambola, papaya, loquat, and palm trees. Each year in July, islanders celebrate Mangomania, a festival held in honor of the tropical fruits that thrive here.

Stringfellow Road crosses a small bridge as it comes into **Bokeelia**, then ends at Main Street, which follows the water's edge on the north end of the island. Fishing is Pine Island's primary recreational activity. The string of fishing piers that extends from the seawall along Main Street attests to that. From here, it's only a twenty-five-minute boat ride northwest to the world-famous Boca Grande Pass tarpon fishing grounds. The waters that surround Pine Island regularly yield snook, cobia, snapper, mackerel, and redfish in addition to tarpon. Technically, we are now on a separate island called Bocilla Island. Jug Creek and small, protected Seagull Bay divide it from Pine Island.

The west end of Main Street dead-ends at Capt'n Con's Fish House. This is the site of Bokeelia's first house, built by H. W. Martin in 1904. The building connected to its west side was Bokeelia's first post office. Martin's wife ran the place as a boardinghouse for boat passengers and fishermen. Now the two-story, wood-frame structure is a popular restaurant.

The Crossed Palms Gallery (see page 156), a block east of Capt'n Con's, is an art lover's wonderland. They have an eclectic collection of paintings, sculpture (metal, glass, clay, and wood), pottery, pop art, and batiks. Owners Nancy and Bob Brooks like to work with undiscovered, exceptionally talented artists. Their collection varies widely from serious to whimsical. There are grand, almost mural-size watercolors in one room and comical, brightly colored ceramic or papier-mâché animal sculptures in the next. I saw a lot of new items on my recent visit. I was fascinated by Terri Causey's brightly painted fish sculptures, wall hangings, and fish furniture. Carole Naster's pink and purple cows are also some of my favorites. David Belling's large, Florida-scene watercolors are as beautiful as I remember from my first visit.

St. James City is at Pine Island's southern extreme. Most of the homes are built on one of the many man-made canals. Stringfellow Road doesn't stop until it hits the seawall at Hopkin's Point, where you'll find the Waterfront Restaurant, housed in St. James City's first schoolhouse. The school building was erected in 1887. It survived a fire in 1896 and was moved twice before settling in its current location. In the late 1940s, it became a fish camp. This is St. James City's busiest eatery. The wood-paneled interior has a rustic, Old Florida feeling. The bar, which was the original school's classroom, has a canoe hanging from the ceiling with hundreds of dollar bills taped to its hull. It looks like an annex of Sloppy Joe's in Key West. I had their outstanding fresh grouper sandwich, which they will prepare seven different ways, from teriyaki-garlic to Jamaican jerk. It's the biggest grouper sandwich I've ever seen—three quarters of a pound of very fresh fish. I had mine "bronzed," grilled with a blend of cinnamon, garlic, and pepper seasoning.

A very good source of information on Pine Island's colorful past is the Museum of the Islands, or MOTI (as the locals call it), just north of the intersection of Stringfellow Road and State Road 78. MOTI has been open since 1990. Some famous names in history have stopped at Pine Island. According to his logs, Ponce de León careened his ship along the western shore in 1513. He and his crew spent several days repairing the ship's hull, gathering wood, and collecting fresh water. He returned to Pine Island in 1521 and, during a skirmish here with the Calusa Indians, was shot with an arrow. His crew took him to Cuba to recuperate, but he died there as a result of his wound.

Much of Pine Island's history predates written record. The Calusa lived on Pine Island for more than a thousand years before Ponce de León came. They built huge shell mounds and dug elaborate canals across the island. It was the arrival of the Spanish that ultimately caused their demise. They had no immunity to European diseases, most notably chickenpox. By the mid-1700s, they were extinct. Remains of their shell mounds still exist on property near the community of **Pineland** on the island's west coast, where the Randall Research Center is located. Scientists at the Center, which is part of the Florida Museum of Natural History, have been conducting an extensive archaeological excavation. They recently began hosting guided tours of the dig (see Appendix for contact information).

The Charlotte Harbor/Pine Island Sound area was a prime haven for pirates. The barrier islands—Sanibel, Captiva, North Captiva, Cayo Costa (or Lacosta), and Gasparilla Island—provided protection from the rougher Gulf seas. The interior islands—Pine Island (the largest), Useppa, and Cabbage Key, along with numerous smaller islands—made ideal hiding places both for their ships and their plunder. Merchant vessels sailing up Florida's west coast, heading for New Orleans, had to pass right by here. British pirate Brewster "Bru" Baker worked these waters and is thought to have lived on Pine Island near present-day Bokeelia. Rumor also says that he buried treasure on Pine Island. Henri Caesar, more widely known as Black Caesar, made his pirate's camp on nearby Sanibel Island.

DIRECTIONS: From I-75, take the North Fort Myers/SR 78 exit (Exit 143). Take SR 78 west.

DON'T MISS: The Crossed Palms Gallery
ADDRESSES AND EVENTS: see page 207–208

SANIBEL AND CAPTIVA

Population: Sanibel 6,064; Captiva 379

HIGHWAY 867 PASSES THROUGH SOUTH FORT MYERS until it reaches the Sanibel Causeway (a $3.00 toll), the only road onto Sanibel and Captiva Islands. The two islands are almost always mentioned in the same breath. They're next to each other, and you must drive through Sanibel to get to Captiva. However, they have quite different personalities.

Sanibel is famous for its gorgeous, shell-strewn beaches and its casual (but still ritzy) boutiques, but there are natural and historic sights as well. At the island's eastern tip, the one-hundred-foot-tall, iron-frame Sanibel Lighthouse has guided ships since its completion in 1884, but it was almost lost before it ever went up. The lighthouse had been built in sections and brought down by ship from New Jersey. Just a few miles

1884 Sanibel Lighthouse

offshore from Sanibel, the ship ran aground and sank. Salvagers, or "wreckers," mostly from Key West, were able to retrieve the sections from the bottom, and construction went forward as planned. It has been a National Landmark since 1972 and is still functional. At the Sanibel Historical Village and Museum, located on Dunlop Road near the intersection of Periwinkle Way and Tarpon Bay Road, you can see a collection of restored 1910s–1930s Sanibel frame houses and buildings.

No doubt Sanibel's best attraction is the J. N. "Ding" Darling National Wildlife Refuge, which occupies six thousand acres on the island's north end (see page 160). Visitors can drive or hike through the refuge and see a wide variety of Florida wildlife, including alligators, turtles, otters, and raccoons. Bird watchers are in heaven here. Several hundred bird species make the refuge their home, among them pink-winged roseate spoonbills, blue herons, white ibis, egrets, owls, and ospreys. The refuge is named after political cartoonist Jay Norwood "Ding" Darling. Darling won a Pulitzer Prize in 1924 and 1943 and later was head of the U.S. Biological Survey and founder of the National Wildlife Foundation. Darling spent his winters on Sanibel and Captiva and championed the cause of conservation and wildlife preservation here long before it was fashionable. As far back as the 1920s, Darling's cartoons reflected his concerns about conservation. It was his efforts that led to Sanibel and Captiva's being declared wildlife sanctuaries by the State of Florida in 1948.

Once you cross the short bridge that spans Blind Pass, which separates the two islands, there is a noticeable shift in topography. **Captiva** is more wildly vegetated, more rustic, quieter, and less populated. It is almost Polynesian in its tropical-ness. Dense flora—sea grapes, frangipani, crotons, spiny aloe, and all varieties of palm including sable, coconut, royal, butterfly, and cabbage—populate the island.

The heart of Captiva is one-block-long Andy Rosse Lane, with the Captiva Island (General) Store at one end and the Mucky Duck, a British pub and restaurant right on the beach, at the other end. In between can be found a variety of odd, little island shops and unusual galleries. Two of my favorites are The Confused Chameleon—knick-knacks, toys, and wacky beach souvenirs in a 1950s cottage—and Jungle Drums Gallery, which features art and sculpture with a wildlife theme. Exceptional restaurants abound on both islands and I couldn't begin to cover them all, but I'll mention a few I always return to. The Sunshine Café, located a half block up Captiva Road from Andy Rosse Lane, is a tiny place with an open-air kitchen that serves outstanding grilled fish and steak entrées and a variety of dishes with a Pan-Asian flare. The Mad Hatter has a terrific view overlooking the beach at Blind Pass. The original Cheeburger Cheeburger on Sanibel has giant, juicy burgers and yummy milkshakes. The Bean on Sanibel (where I have to get my coffee fix every morning) also offers breakfast, bagels, pastries, and muffins. And don't forget the Mucky Duck.

Two of my favorite getaways are here. The Castaways sits just across Blind Pass on the Sanibel side. Nothing fancy, just simple 1940s- and '50s-era, wood-frame beach cottages and duplex cottages with screen porches and slanting floors. Ten of the thirty units are right on the beach. The 'Tween Waters Inn is in the middle of Captiva, near its narrowest point between the Gulf of Mexico and Pine Island Sound. The inn has been a fixture here for three quarters of a century.

Captiva's first settlers arrived in the late 1800s and early 1900s, long after the pirates who frequented these waters had been vanquished. One settler was Dr. J. Dickey from Bristol, Virginia. Dickey visited Captiva on a fishing trip in 1900, then returned with his family in 1905. Since there were no schools on Captiva, Dickey also brought along a tutor for his children named Miss Reba Fitzpatrick. He built a schoolhouse with living quarters for Miss Reba upstairs. Mr. and Mrs. Bowman Price, friends of the Dickeys from Bristol, purchased the schoolhouse and surrounding property in 1925. In 1931, they converted the old school into the 'Tween Waters Inn. Over the years, the Prices added cottages to accommodate new visitors who arrived every winter. In the late 1940s, they floated army barracks across the sound from Fort Myers to add more cottages.

Some famous people made the 'Tween Waters their winter retreat. Anne Morrow Lindbergh, prolific author and wife of Charles Lindbergh, stayed here in the 1950s. She wrote one of her best known works, *Gift from the Sea*, while on Captiva. Cartoonist "Ding" Darling frequented the 'Tween Waters too. He would rent two cottages: #103 as his room and #105 as his studio.

Chapel by the Sea, Captiva

Do a little back roads exploring on Captiva and you'll eventually run across the Chapel by the Sea. Captiva's earliest settler, William Binder, built the tiny, white chapel on Chapin Road in 1901 as a schoolhouse. Binder was shipwrecked off Captiva in 1885 and was the first to file a homestead claim on the island. Next to the Chapel by the Sea is the Captiva Cemetery, shaded by gumbo-limbo trees. The high spot shared by the chapel and cemetery is an ancient Calusa Indian shell midden.

DIRECTIONS: From I-75, take the Highway 884 exit (Exit 135) west to Highway 867. Travel southwest on Highway 867 to the Sanibel Causeway.

DON'T MISS: The J. N. "Ding" Darling National Wildlife Refuge
ADDRESSES AND EVENTS: see page 208–209

ESTERO

Population: 9,503

THE ESTERO (SPANISH FOR ESTUARY) RIVER CROSSES beneath Highway 41 just north of County Road 850. Estero River Outfitters has been located here since 1977. One of its most popular guided kayak trips is a five-mile paddle downriver and out to Mound Key.

Mound Key was a thriving Calusa Indian village known as Calos when Spanish explorers first ran across it nearly five hundred years ago. The Calusa and their ancestors had populated this region for fifteen hundred years prior to that, but they died out by the mid-1700s from exposure to European diseases to which they had no immunity. Three thirty-foot-high shell mounds rise from Mound Key's center, the only obvious reminders that the Calusa were there.

On the way out to Mound Key, paddlers pass by the scenic grounds of the Koreshan State Historic Site, the setting for one of the oddest chapters in Florida history. In 1869, Dr. Cyrus Teed, a medical doctor living near Syracuse, New York, experienced what he labeled "an illu-mination, a vision." Teed had recently become disgruntled with conven-tional medicine and had begun studying metaphysics. During this illu-mination, according to Teed, a list of universal truths was revealed to him by an angel. Following that experience, he felt compelled to form an organization based on what he had divined. His initial attempts in New York failed, but in 1886 in Chicago, he generated enough of a fol-lowing to incorporate his so-called College of Life. Two years later, he opened a communal home there where his followers could reside. Cyrus Teed adopted the name Koresh (which is ancient Hebrew for Cyrus). His organization evolved into the Koreshan Unity, and his doctrine became known as Koreshanity. In 1894, Teed purchased three hundred acres along the Estero River from German immigrant Gustave Damkohler (one of the earliest settlers in what is now Estero) on which to begin building a communal "New Jerusalem." Dr. Teed envisioned an enormous, hub-shaped city, large enough to be home to ten million peo-ple. His detailed plan included such far-thinking ideas as underground passageways to carry out refuse, which would then be recycled and returned as compost.

Of course, the plan never came to fruition. People who visit here reg-ularly comment, "Is it any wonder that they died out? They didn't believe in reproducing!" This is a common misunderstanding. It's true that Dr. Teed and the Koreshans believed in a celibate lifestyle but only for those who worked full-time in the leadership, governing, and oper-ation of the commune. These people lived in separate dormitories, while Koreshans who had families lived in outlying cottages. Teed counted on outside recruits to grow their numbers.

Teed's beliefs had some basis in Christianity, although he believed that the Bible was written symbolically and required the interpretation of a prophet. Koreshanity mixed theological, sociological, and (sup-posed) scientific theories into one philosophy. One of his most bizarre beliefs was something called "Cellular Cosmogony," which purported that the surface of the Earth was on the inside of a giant sphere, and that the sun (which revolved and had both a light and a dark side), the planets, and space existed in the center of that sphere. Teed was so intent on convincing the scientific community that this was indeed the case that he staged an experiment to prove it. The Koreshan Unity's "geodetic" staff constructed an enormous accordion-like contraption, which they named the "Rectilineater," to prove their hypothesis. It stretched out from the beach into Estero Bay. No one really seems to understand exactly what it was supposed to measure, but the geodetic staff claimed that it substantiated their theory. They were so confident in their findings that they offered $10,000 to anyone who could disprove them. Apparently no one ever bothered to challenge them.

Granted, there were some peculiarities about these folks, but unlike most other religious cults and communes, the Koreshans were inclusive. They interacted happily with and were a part of the surrounding communities. They always welcomed outsiders and never condemned others for disagreeing with their doctrine. They were also very industrious people. They farmed citrus, shipped fruit, operated printing presses, and ran a sawmill, a boat-building business, a general store, a bakery, and eventually a restaurant. They even had their own well-known and popular concert band. The Koreshan Unity continued to acquire property and in 1904 owned about seventy-five hundred acres.

Cyrus "Koresh" Teed died in 1908, and the Koreshan Unity's population began a slow decline. In 1961, the handful of remaining Koreshans donated the Koreshan Unity property to the State of Florida to become a state historic site. Hedwig Michel was the last president of the Koreshan Unity and the last living Koreshan. She died in 1982 at age ninety.

The Koreshan State Historic Site rests on the 305 donated acres on the east side of Highway 41 between Corkscrew Road and the Estero River. Across the highway is the headquarters for the Koreshan Unity Foundation, a nonprofit organization whose purpose is to preserve the Koreshan's historical heritage. Most important, they are the keepers of all the original Koreshan archives. The circular-shaped headquarters building is architecturally striking in a Frank Lloyd Wright-ish kind of way. It triples as the foundation's offices, library, and museum. No employees at the foundation are Koreshan. In other words, they do not believe that we live on the inside of the earth. Their interest stems strictly from a historical preservation standpoint.

Shelves of books from Teed's personal library fill several walls. A few of the books are so old that no one will even attempt to open them. Pictures cover the rest of the walls—old photographs that document daily Koreshan life as well as paintings by Douglas Arthur Teed, Cyrus Teed's son (who was born, presumably, prior to Dr. Teed's commitment to celibacy). Interestingly, Douglas, an accomplished artist who studied in Europe, chose not to be a Koreshan. The foundation has also collected furniture and artifacts that belonged to the Koreshan Unity, including many items from Dr. Teed's residence, among them his folding Murphy bed. Teed loved music and encouraged its teaching, and his piano and organ are also on display here.

Many of the original buildings have been restored, and the grounds appear much as they did one hundred years ago. Among the restored buildings are Dr. Teed's two-story house (the "Founder's House"), built in 1896 and the oldest standing original-settlement building; the "New Store," built in the early 1920s and containing a general store, post office, and restaurant that catered to passing traffic on Tamiami Trail (Highway 41); and the "Planetary Court," built in 1904 and painted bright yellow with green trim. This is where the women of the Planetary Chamber, the Koreshan's day-to-day governing council, lived and maintained their offices. Henry Silverfriend, the women's guardian, lived in its roof-top apartment. The 1905 Arts Hall (under renovation when I last visited) was the Koreshans' social and community center. Now it serves as a museum that features a model of the Rectilineater along with photographs and paintings. One large painting depicts an aerial view of the anticipated New Jerusalem. There is also a globe that demonstrates the theory of Cellular Cosmogony.

The Koreshans and their beliefs may have died out, but the remains of their odd world and existence have been well preserved by the Koreshan Unity Foundation and the Koreshan State Historic Site.

DIRECTIONS: From I-75, take the CR 850/Corkscrew Road exit (Exit 123) west 2 miles.

DON'T MISS: The Koreshan State Historic Site
ADDRESSES AND EVENTS: see page 209

EVERGLADES CITY, CHOKOLOSKEE, AND OCHOPEE

Population: Everglades City 479; Chokoloskee 404; Ochopee 128

THERE ARE REALLY ONLY TWO SEASONS IN THE EVERGLADES: mosquito and non-mosquito, which roughly coincide with the wet and dry seasons. Non-mosquito/dry is from December through March. Those who live here year-round are hardy souls indeed, and they live in an amazing, other-worldly place. Speedy passersby on Alligator Alley (I-75 from Naples to Fort Lauderdale) or the Tamiami Trail (Highway 41 to Miami) miss much of what the Everglades is all about.

It would be blasphemy to bring up the word "Everglades" without mentioning Marjory Stoneman Douglas, author of *The Everglades: River of Grass*. She coined the phrase "river of grass," which refers to the fact that the Everglades requires a flow of water from lakes to the north for its survival. Water evaporating from the Everglades supplies much of the state's rainfall. Douglas was among the first to recognize and publicize the importance of the Everglades and the fragility of its ecological balance. Her book was published in 1947, the same year Everglades National Park was created and long before the term "environmentalist" could be found in the dictionary. Since then, she fought vigorously against human encroachment on the Everglades. In the 1960s, while in her late seventies, she became involved with the Audubon Society of Miami's efforts to combat the building of a jetport in the Everglades. Society members pleaded with her to start an organization that would unite the efforts of those concerned with the fate the Everglades. She did and named it Friends of the Everglades, an organization that is, today, one of the most powerful voices for the area's preservation.

The primary source for the "river of grass" is Lake Okeechobee. Tributaries fan out from the south end of the lake and spread across the bottom of the state. With only a fifteen-foot drop in elevation from Okeechobee to Florida Bay, the flow is nearly imperceptible, and although most of the Everglades is underwater, it is seldom more than a foot deep. A chunk of the west central portion is designated the Big Cypress National Preserve. Everglades National Park actually encompasses only about the lower fifth of the entire Everglades, but that's still 1.4 million acres. To look at it from Alligator Alley or the Tamiami Trail, it seems to be just an endless expanse of sawgrass, dotted with an occasional slash pine bay head, all the way to the horizon. Closer observation reveals that it's brimming with wildlife.

If you stand in one place long enough, there's a good chance you'll see great blue herons, great egrets (or their smaller cousins, snowy egrets), perhaps a wood ibis (a type of stork), or an anhinga, which some refer to as a snakebird because it swims with only its head and neck above water. You might also see a pink roseate spoonbill or maybe a purple gallinule, whose big feet have evolved such that this little bird can walk on top of floating lily pads without sinking. One of the most colorful birds in the Everglades, the gallinule has iridescent green wing feathers and a bluish-purple neck and head. Ospreys and bald eagles also call the Everglades home. The very rare Everglades kite, or snail kite, lives here too and feeds exclusively on apple snails.

There's far less chance that you'll see a Florida panther, our state mammal, although this is its natural habitat. Park rangers estimate that there are perhaps only seventy or eighty of these beautiful animals left. It's also unlikely that you'll see any of the few crocodiles that live in the southeast section of the park. Everglades National Park is the only place in the United States where they coexist with their broader-snouted relatives, alligators. I can almost guarantee that you will see alligators. Placed on the Endangered Species List in the late 1960s, these prehistoric reptiles made an astounding comeback and were removed from the list in 1987. Now you can hardly set foot in the Everglades without stepping on one. Armadillos, opossums, and otters are some of the Everglades' other residents.

As amazing as all this fauna is, it's only one-tenth of the wildlife that you would have seen here forty years ago. The continuing population explosion along south Florida's coast—and all the development that comes with it—has siphoned off the lifeblood of the Everglades and wreaked ecological havoc. Today, its wetland area is less than half its original size.

It's a straight, three-mile shot south on Highway 29, off Highway 41, through mangrove swamp to **Everglades City**. You'll pass signs that read "Speedy Johnson's Airboat Rides," "Captain Doug House's Airboat Tours," "Gator Airboat Tours," and "Jungle Erv's Airboat Rides." It seems like everybody and his Aunt Mildred are in the airboat tour business down here. Except for those that park rangers use for patrolling, airboats aren't allowed in Everglades National Park. They are, however, allowed in the Big Cypress National Preserve. Everglades City sits on the border between the two, so the airboat tours go north, east, or west.

Highway 29 crosses a bridge at the Barron River, and Everglades City is on the other side. It's a sleepy, little fishing community with a full-time population of fewer than five hundred. This was industrialist Barron G. Collier's company town from the 1920s through the 1950s. It was an active shipping port for south Florida produce and commercial seafood. It was also the county seat. After Hurricane Donna ravaged the area in 1960, Collier pulled his interests out. The county seat moved to Naples, and Everglades City settled into the quiet fishing village it is today. The homes in the center of town are mostly small, pastel-colored slat-wood cottages. All have at least one old boat—up on blocks and in some stage of disrepair—in their side yards.

Speedy Johnson's, a couple of boat-repair shops, a wholesale seafood house, and an open lot stacked ten feet high with crab traps all border the Barron River on the town's east side. Staying on 29, follow the water's edge on the west side and you'll pass a few tourist shops and the Oarhouse Restaurant on the right. The Oarhouse is a good spot for local cuisine. The house platter is "cooter, legs, and tail," which is turtle, frog legs, and gator tail. A couple more blocks further south is the town square, which is actually a circle. Here you'll find the Museum of the Everglades in the recently restored (1997) Historic Laundry Building. Built in 1927, it was one of Barron Collier's company town buildings and remained a commercial laundry through World War II. In 2001, it was added to the National Register of Historic Places. The museum opened in 1998. A collection of Calusa and Seminole artifacts, as well as old photographs chronicling the town's evolution, are on permanent display. Also included is some of the original laundry equipment dating back to the 1940s, including a centrifugal dry cleaner. There are also rotating displays of the works of local artists, artisans, and photographers.

Front entrance at the Rod & Gun Club, Everglades City

Two blocks east of the circle is the Rod and Gun Club, a white, three-story, clapboard lodge overlooking the Barron River. Yellow and white awnings hang out over its windows and entrances. Everglades City founder W. S. Allen built the original building in 1850. When Allen passed away in 1889, George W. Storter bought the lodge from Allen's estate, along with most of the surrounding property that comprised Everglades City. Storter paid only $800 for it. He enlarged the lodge to accommodate the hunters, sport fishermen, and yachting parties coming to the Everglades in increasing numbers each winter season. In 1922, Barron G. Collier took over and operated it as a private club for his fellow industrial magnates and political dignitaries. Herbert Hoover, Franklin D. Roosevelt, Dwight Eisenhower, and Richard Nixon have all been guests at the Rod and Gun Club.

Framed newspaper articles and photographs of famous visitors cover the walls in the hallway that leads to the lobby from the parking lot. One photo shows a proud Robert Rand next to his trophy catch: a seven-and-a-half-foot, 187-pound tarpon caught in March 1939. Another is of Dwight and Mamie Eisenhower. Dwight is wearing shorts and a scruffy fishing hat. The grin on his face and the long rack of fish behind him indicate that he must have had a big day. The lobby is a trophy room. Ernest Hemingway would have felt right at home here. A five-foot-long sawfish bill, a gaping shark's jaw, a stretched alligator hide, deer and wild boar heads, and an assortment of game fish festoon the dark, wood-paneled walls. A pool table and an upright saloon piano occupy one end of the room. A large open fireplace sits in the middle, though I can't imagine it getting cold enough here to use it. The lobby opens onto the dining room, which is an even bigger trophy room, with tarpon, barracuda, snook, lobster, and what looks like the shell of a very old, giant sea turtle hanging on the wall. A stuffed raccoon keeps an eye on guests from its permanent perch behind the registration desk.

Highway 29 continues south towards Chokoloskee. From the road all you can see, west and south, are swamp and mangrove islands all the way to the horizon. Much has been written and said about how easy it is to become permanently lost in this massive maze. Common stories around here begin with the line, "They set out from here into the Glades and were never seen again." One mangrove island looks a lot like the next. It's easy to imagine someone paddling aimlessly out there for days, or even weeks, before succumbing to dehydration. The alligators would take care of their funeral. . . .

In **Chokoloskee** there's a small marina on the left and the Chokoloskee Mall a little further up on the right. The mall consists of Captain J. Carlisle's Tackle Box and Guide Service, Carla's Grocery, and the post office. Just beyond the mall, turn right onto East Chokoloskee Road, then left onto Mamie Street, which dead-ends at the historic Smallwood Store.

If Everglades City is sleepy, then Chokoloskee is positively comatose, but that's its charm. It was commonly referred to as the "Big Island," but *chokoloskee* is a mixture of Seminole words that roughly translate to "old abandoned house." Archaeologists tell us that coastal mound dwellers inhabited Chokoloskee and the surrounding islands more than two thousand years ago, possibly as far back as ten thousand years. These inhabitants left relics remarkably similar to those left by Central American Mayans, which has led to speculation that they may have communicated with and traded with the Mayans. More recently, Chokoloskee was a refuge for the Seminole Indians forced out of central Florida during the Seminole Wars. Chief Billy Bowlegs lived here in the mid-1800s.

About the same time W. S. Allen was developing Everglades City, Ted Smallwood was settling Chokoloskee. He began farming there in 1896, and in 1906 he turned his home into a trading post that grew into a full-time store and post office. Ted traded with the Seminoles, fishermen, fur traders, and other early settlers on the island. By 1917, the store had outgrown his house, so he built a larger facility down on the water's edge. In 1924, a violent storm blew four feet of water into the store and actually shifted its foundation. The following year, Ted raised the building up on wooden pilings, just in time to weather the severe 1926 hurricane.

In 1974, the Smallwood Store was placed on the National Register of Historic Places. It was still an active store up until 1982. Lynn Smallwood, Ted's granddaughter, owns it now. In 1990, she began restoring the tin-sided, tin-roofed building as a museum.

From the front door, you can see straight through the length of the store to the back door and the porch, which looks out over the water. The interior of the store looks much the same as it did for the better part of the twentieth century. Wall shelves hold staple goods and supplies that were typical of the store's inventory. A life-size likeness of Ted Smallwood sits in his favorite rocking chair. With his bushy mustache, tall hat, and glasses, he could be Teddy Roosevelt's twin. The store's original furnishings are still here. There's a long counter that runs the length of one wall with old books and photographs from Chokoloskee's bygone era on display. Decades of elbows leaning on the countertop have worn its edge smooth and rounded. Thousands of old mud dauber nests cover the ceiling. The store has been restored, but (except for Ted) it is not a re-creation. This is the real thing.

The museum devotes part of a side room to the life story of one of this area's most interesting characters. Totch Brown lived near here for three quarters of a century. He made a living as a fisherman and gator trapper and even admitted to having been an occasional marijuana smuggler in the early 1970s.

Leaving Everglades City behind, turn east onto Highway 41/Tamiami Trail and keep an eye out for the famous **Ochopee** Post Office about four miles down the road on the right. It's a corrugated tin shed, hardly bigger than an outhouse, that has the distinction of being the smallest official post office in the United States. The tiny

Ochopee Post Office on the Tamiami Trail

building was originally an irrigation pipe shed for a tomato farm. A 1953 fire burned Ochopee's previous general store and post office to the ground. Postmaster Sidney Brown hurriedly put the pipe shed into temporary service. It served its purpose so well that no one saw reason to replace it, and ever since it has been in continuous service as the post office and Trailways bus ticket station. Tourists stop here regularly just to get the Ochopee 34141 postmark on their mail.

Another eighteen miles east will bring you to Clyde Butcher's Big Cypress Gallery on the right. Clyde Butcher is Florida's answer to Ansel Adams. His spectacular, large-format, black-and-white photographs—most of them scenic Florida landscapes—have been displayed around the world.

DIRECTIONS: From Highway 41/Tamiami Trail, turn south onto SR 29 (25 miles southeast of Naples) to Everglades City. Continue south another four miles to Chokoloskee. Ochopee is 29 miles southeast of Naples on Highway 41/Tamiami Trail.

DON'T MISS: The Rod and Gun Club, Historic Ted Smallwood's Store, and the Clyde Butcher Gallery
ADDRESSES AND EVENTS: see page 209–210

TAVERNIER AND ISLAMORADA

Population: 6,846

THE FLORIDA KEYS, A ONE-HUNDRED-MILE-LONG STRING of islands, begins less than an hour south of Miami, but these islands are philosophically a lifetime away from that congested metropolis. U.S. Highway 1 is Florida's bridge to the Caribbean. The Keys could be its own country. Key West tried secession in 1982, when a Federal drug-search roadblock jammed all traffic to and from the islands. The frustrated town proclaimed its independence from the United States and adopted the name "Conch Republic."

Three pioneer families—the Russells, the Pinders, and the Parkers—sailed to Upper Matecumbe Key (Islamorada) in the mid and late 1800s from the Bahamas. These Anglo-Bahamian settlers were called "Conchs," after the shellfish that was such a staple in their diet. They built their homes from driftwood, planted pineapple and Key lime groves, and fished. In 1905, their island outpost became connected with the rest of civilization when Henry Flagler built his railroad through here on its way to Key West. Several hotels and vacation homes were built on Islamorada. The Tavernier Hotel went up in Tavernier (it's still there), and Flagler built a fishing camp just south, on Long Key.

The Keys sit along the only living coral reef in the continental United States and offer some of the best fishing and scuba diving in the world. Tavernier and Islamorada, two middle north–end Keys towns that blend into one, typify the communities that dot U.S. Highway 1. Less "touristy" than their neighbors—Key Largo to the immediate north and Key West eighty miles south—Tavernier and Islamorada offer as their main attractions fishing, scuba diving, snorkeling, and dining on fresh seafood. It's difficult to get off the beaten path down here since there is only one path (Highway 1). However, this makes it easy to give directions using mile markers. Add two digits to the end of the mile marker number and that's the street address.

The Green Turtle Inn is at mile marker 81.5. In 1947, Sid and Roxie Siderious opened their roadside diner specializing in locally fished turtle made into soups and steaks. At that time, sea turtles were plentiful in the Keys, but in a few short decades, their population was decimated. Fishing for sea turtles was finally outlawed in the 1970s. Now the restaurant serves freshwater turtle bought from turtle farms near Lake Okeechobee.

I've had the Green Turtle Inn's turtle soup before and it's good. I also like their conch salad. The conch is a large mollusk native to these waters, Florida's answer to California's abalone. Typically, the meat is rather chewy and must be cut into thin strips to eat. The Green Turtle Inn's comes in a tomato-based marinade with onions and green and red peppers.

The Green Turtle Inn's owner is Henry Rosenthal, a magician who performs around the world. His stage name is Bastille. One room at the restaurant is dedicated to famous magicians. Posters and autographed glossy photos of David Copperfield and Harry Blackstone, among others, cover the walls. Sometimes Bastille performs impromptu for his dinner patrons. One of the waiters told me, "Mr. Rosenthal is a terrific entertainer, but I wouldn't want to play him at cards."

Manny & Isa's Kitchen, at mile marker 81.6, is just a few blocks north. Manny Ortiz immigrated to the Florida Keys from Cuba in 1955. Not long after, he met and married Isa. They opened their restaurant in 1965. It's a cozy place with only nine tables. They serve outstanding Cuban and Spanish dishes and the best homemade Key lime pie in the world. A lofty claim, I know, but it's true. To make his much-in-demand pies, Manny squeezes six to seven thousand of the diminutive limes per year. It takes about two hundred limes to get one gallon of juice. Key limes are smaller but juicier than standard limes. These come from his own grove. I've tried Key lime pie all over the state of Florida—at the best restaurants in Tampa, Orlando, Miami, and Key West—but I've never had any that even comes close to Manny's. It's the best. It's dense and sweet. The meringue actually has flavor, not just air. His crust is the flaky dough variety, not graham cracker. I savor each bite and complement it with a rich cup of Cuban *café con leche.*

Just north of Manny & Isa's you'll find the 1935 Hurricane

1935 Hurricane Monument, Islamorada

Monument at mile marker 81.8. It's also a tomb that contains the cremated remains of some of the storm's victims. A plaque at the base of the twelve-foot-tall coral keystone monolith reads, "Dedicated to the memory of the civilians and war veterans whose lives were lost in the hurricane of September Second 1935."

Directly across the street from the monument, the Helen Wadley Branch Library occupies what was originally a storm shelter built by the Red Cross and the Works Progress Administration (WPA) immediately after the 1935 Hurricane. The library's tiny sign and nondescript concrete building make it difficult to spot, but for those with an interest in Keys history, particularly in the 1935 Hurricane, this is the place to come. On my first visit, the librarian directed me to a back room where file cabinets are filled with copies of new and old magazine and newspaper articles, including some written by Ernest Hemingway. There's no better place to spend an afternoon.

I was searching for information about the hurricane, but, rummaging through the library's files, I found lots of bits and pieces that sidetracked me. There are quite a few articles about Zane Grey, known by most as the famous writer of Western novels. What is less widely known about him is that he was a fanatical sport fisherman and that he actually invented much of the light tackle and fishing techniques that sportfishing enthusiasts still use today.

At the turn of the century, sailfish were considered a nuisance to Keys fishermen, who were more interested in hunting king mackerel or tarpon. Called spikefish or boohoos, the big, sleek sailfish were crafty at stealing bait, and only a couple of people had managed to actually catch one. In 1910, Zane and his brother Romer were on their way to Mexico to fish for tarpon when they got word of a yellow fever outbreak there. They diverted to the Florida Keys and Henry Flagler's Long Key Fishing Camp, about ten miles south of modern-day Islamorada. The Greys went after the sailfish with a passion. They used light tackle, which made battles all the more monumental! The fierce-fighting and long-leaping sailfish rapidly gained a reputation as the ultimate sportfish.

The Long Key Fishing Camp was a popular destination frequented by society's elite: William Randolph Hearst, Herbert Hoover, Franklin D. Roosevelt, and William Vanderbilt. Its attractiveness all came to a sudden end, however, on September 2, 1935. Most people assume that 1992's Hurricane Andrew was the most powerful storm to hit the United States in the twentieth century. As devastating as it was, there was one that surpassed it in strength.

On September 1, 1935, locals on the Lower and Upper Matecumbe Keys were boarding up their homes in preparation for a tropical storm that was crossing the Bahamas. Weather forecasters were predicting that it would pass south of Key West, but by the morning of September 2, Labor Day, barometers on the Matecumbe Keys were dropping rapidly. That meant that the storm had veered northeast and was gaining strength.

In the summer of 1935, the Veterans Administration had sent 680 unemployed World War I veterans to the upper Keys to build roads and bridges. The press referred to them as "bonus-marching veterans" because they had marched on Washington, D.C., to protest that they could not get jobs after returning from the war and wanted their war bonuses accelerated. The roadwork veterans were living in three construction camps on Upper and Lower Matecumbe Keys. About two thirds of them had gone to Miami or Key West for that Labor Day holiday. Those who remained met a horrible fate.

By nightfall, the winds were howling, and it was apparent that this would be a big one. Families huddled in their wood-frame "Conch" bungalows and storm shelters. At 8:30 P.M., the barometer read an all-time Northern hemisphere record low pressure of 26.35 millibars.

The hurricane cut a swath right through Upper Matecumbe. Winds blew to 260 miles per hour. A twenty-foot tidal wave swept over the islands, ripping whole houses, with families in them, off their foundations. Roger Albury and his nine family members were in their eight-room Tavernier house when the wave picked it up and carried it over two hundred feet.

Seventeen-year-old Bernard Russell and his family sought shelter in his father's Islamorada lime packinghouse. When flood waters came pouring in, they tried to escape to higher ground. Clinging desperately to each other, they pushed out of the packinghouse and were instantly blown apart. Bernard's sister and his young nephew were torn from his hands. Of the sixty members of the extended Russell family, only eleven survived the hurricane.

Earlier in the day, an eleven-car passenger train had left Miami to try to evacuate the upper Keys residents and the war veteran road workers. It reached Islamorada right when the wall of water struck, blasting each of the one-hundred-ton passenger cars right off the tracks. Only the locomotive remained upright. It was the last train to travel these tracks. Flagler never rebuilt his railroad.

Ultimately, 408 bodies were counted, but the actual death toll was probably twice that. All of the war veteran road workers who had stayed on the islands were killed. Months after the storm, remains of victims' bodies were still being recovered. Thirty years later, while dredging on an outlying key near Islamorada, a developer found an automobile with 1935 license plates and five skeletons inside.

I found a scathing newspaper editorial entitled "Who Murdered the Vets?" written on September 17, 1935, by Ernest Hemingway. Hemingway was living in Key West at the time and had gone to the upper Keys with crews to assist in the rescue efforts two days after the disaster. His article was an angry indictment of the newly formed Veterans Administration for sending the veterans down to the Keys to work during the most dangerous time of year—hurricane season. It reads in part, ". . . fishermen such as President Herbert Hoover, and President Roosevelt, do not come to the Florida Keys in hurricane months. . . . There is a known danger to property. . . . But veterans, especially the bonus-marching variety, are not property. They are only human beings; unsuccessful human beings, and all they have to lose are their lives. They are doing coolie labor, for a top wage of $45 a month, and they have been put down on the Florida Keys where they can't make trouble."

The long and painful process of rebuilding began immediately after the storm had passed and the bodies were buried. Young Bernard Russell, who had seen his family all but wiped out, remained on the island. He started his own cabinet-building/carpentry business and later founded Islamorada's first fire rescue department. In a 1991 *St. Petersburg Times* interview, he said, "The thing I have always asked myself is this: 'Why was I spared? Why am I still here?' I saw great big robust he-men, dead on the ground. I saw little skinny children who survived. How do you put that together in your mind? I have to think the Lord might have a purpose for me. I might be needed."

One of Tavernier's oldest structures is the historic Tavernier Hotel at mile marker 91.8. This pink and peach concrete-block, two-story hotel was built in 1928. It was one of the few buildings that survived the 1935 hurricane. Try the fish (mahi-mahi) and grits for breakfast at the Copper Kettle Restaurant next door.

The Cheeca Lodge, at mile marker 82 on the Atlantic side, is an elegant but understated resort. Norman Schwarzkopf and George Bush Sr. stay here when they come to Islamorada to fish. It's a beautiful place, but even if you don't stay here, go see the Pioneer Cemetery.

Among the first buildings that the Conchs built on Islamorada were a schoolhouse (1900) and a church (1890), on property that is now part of the Cheeca Lodge compound. Next to the church, they established a small cemetery. The 1935 hurricane destroyed the schoolhouse and the church, but the cemetery remains.

Looking out of place among the beach loungers and rental Hobie Cats, the tiny cemetery is surrounded by a low, white picket fence. Only eleven gravesites are marked; there are some more without names. In the center, a life-size statue of an angel marks the grave of Etta Dolores Pinder (1899–1914). Tossed a thousand feet in the mighty winds of the

1935 hurricane, the angel, with one wing broken and a hand missing, nevertheless stands tall. A historical marker in one corner of the cemetery reads: "This cemetery memorializes the determination and vision of over fifty pioneer Anglo-Bahamian Conchs who labored to settle and organize the first community on Matecumbe Key. Descendants of three pioneer families, the Russells who homesteaded in 1854, the Pinders in 1873, and the Parkers in 1898, are buried on this land."

DIRECTIONS: Tavernier is 67 miles south of Miami on Highway 1. Continue 12 more miles south to Islamorada.

DON'T MISS: The Key lime pie at Manny & Isa's Kitchen in Islamorada

ADDRESSES AND EVENTS: see page 210

BIG PINE KEY AND NO NAME KEY

Population: 5,032

BIG PINE KEY, THE LARGEST ISLAND in the lower keys, could be Florida's answer to the Galapagos Islands. Along with its northwest appendage, No Name Key, it is home to a number of rare and endangered birds, reptiles, and mammals—including the seldom-sighted, short-eared Lower Keys marsh rabbit (rumored to actually swim between the islands occasionally). **Big Pine Key**'s best-known and most-endangered inhabitant is the petite Key, or toy, deer. Key deer are the smallest race of North American deer and are endemic to the Lower Keys; nearly the entire population is found on Big Pine and No Name Keys. A typical adult weighs between forty and seventy pounds and stands less than two and half feet tall at the shoulder. Disproportionately large ears and brown eyes add considerably to the deer's "cuteness" quotient. Unfortunately, their adorableness may be one of the factors contributing to their demise.

Commercial development did not take place on Big Pine Key (except for a little joint called the No Name Pub) until the late 1960s, but there have been small settlements here and on No Name Key for over a hundred years. Some of the people who lived here in the mid-1800s were fishermen and spongers, but most were here to harvest buttonwood trees (found in the lower and wetter areas of the island) for charcoal.

Just thirty-five miles south, Key West, the most populous city in Florida in the mid-1800s and the richest per capita, was experiencing its Golden Era. Big Pine Key charcoal was much in demand as a fuel source. Early (1500s) Spanish explorers had called Key West *Cayo Hueso*, which means "Island of Bones," presumably because they found piles of bones left there from some long-ago Calusa Indian battle. A couple of centuries later, the moniker was still appropriate, considering that Key West's biggest money crop in the 1800s was the remains (or bones, if you will) of ships smashed on the surrounding reefs. This perfectly legal industry was called wrecking, and brave Key Westers were making a mint salvaging the cargoes of wrecked ships. Wrecking created both an industrial boom and a population boom in Key West, and that kept Big Pine Key's charcoal industry burning. But nothing lasts forever.

At the end of the nineteenth century, with the construction of lighthouses in the Lower Keys to warn ships away from reefs, the wrecking industry died a quick death. Big Pine Key's buttonwood charcoal business—and the settlements that had resulted from it—soon followed suit.

In 1905, Henry Flagler started building his Overseas Railroad and began connecting the dots of the Keys. It rolled across Big Pine Key around 1909 or 1910 and finished in Key West in 1912. The Labor Day Hurricane of 1935—the largest ever to strike Florida—brought an end to the Overseas Railroad when it ripped across the Upper Keys, blasting an entire train sent by Flagler to rescue road workers on Islamorada right off the tracks. (See the Tavernier and Islamorada section.)

By 1938, the Overseas Highway had been paved to Key West, reusing many of Flagler's railway bridges, but Big Pine Key and No Name Key were largely unaffected. Their few inhabitants were mostly fishermen or rumrunners left over from the Prohibition era and seeking anonymity.

In 1957, the U. S. Fish and Wildlife Service established the National Key Deer Refuge on Big Pine and No Name Keys. Hunters had decimated the Key deer population: There were fewer than fifty deer in 1949. First refuge manager and local hero Jack Watson fought vehemently for their survival and is credited with saving them, almost single-handedly, from extinction. He battled poachers like the sheriff in a Wild West town, sometimes resorting to sinking their boats and torching their pickup trucks. Watson retired in 1975, and three years later the Key deer reached its population peak of four hundred.

Sadly, those numbers declined over the following two decades. Loss of habitat, unusually low birth rates (Key deer rarely have multiple births) and automobile strikes are the most often-cited reasons. When I visited Big Pine Key and No Name Key in 1998, there were fewer than three hundred deer left on the islands (counted in 1997). Recently, however, there has been significant progress in the effort to bolster the Key deer's population. The most recent count puts their numbers at over six hundred. Despite this improvement, they are still at great risk. More than half of those that die each year are killed by automobile strikes. Hand-feeding exacerbates the problem. These little guys are so cute that people get out of their cars to feed them. The deer are quick learners, and before long they start running out to cars—and invariably get hit. The fine for feeding a Key deer is $250.

Publicizing the National Key Deer Refuge is a double-edged sword: the value of an increased awareness of the Key deer's plight weighed against the potential for more traffic. Every person I spoke to in the community said something to me about driving slowly and carefully (whether I asked about it or not). The local police do their part. They write speeding tickets for just one mile per hour over the limit, which is 35 M.P.H. almost everywhere on the islands.

The architecturally eclectic Barnacle Bed & Breakfast on Big Pine Key,
designed and built by Steven "Woody" Cornell in 1976

Big Pine Key is decidedly quieter and more leisurely than its famous neighbor to the south. A great place to stay is the Barnacle Bed and Breakfast, where leisure has been refined to an art form. Long Beach Road dead-ends a short ways past it, so there is no traffic. A simple limestone wall marks the entrance. The Barnacle is an architectural enigma. Its style doesn't fall neatly into any conventional category. Modern, eclectic, nautical, tropical—there are no right angles. Its pipe railings, archways, and generous open-air balcony remind me, more than anything else, of an ocean liner, albeit with an exterior painted in varying shades of earth tones reminiscent of the 1970s. From the top-floor sunrise-watching deck (the ocean liner's bow), guests can scan the Atlantic's vivid turquoise water for rolling dolphin or maybe a jumping manta ray.

Original owner Steven "Woody" Cornell designed and built the Barnacle in 1976. Dive operators Tim and Jane Marquis bought it from Woody in 1994. I've stayed in their downstairs Ocean Room (done in shades of pastel sea green and plum), which opens directly onto the beach. Multicolored hexagonal tiles cover the floor. Creative use of space for the bathroom, the kitchenette, and shelving reminds me of a stateroom on the *Queen Elizabeth*. Again, the walls are skewed at odd angles, and the floor plan is a series of triangles. The bed sits in its own little alcove that faces the coconut palm–lined beach and the ocean through sliding glass doors.

A likely place to spot wildlife is Big Pine Key's Blue Hole. Back in the 1930s, road construction crews mined the hard oolitic limestone that makes up Big Pine Key. They extracted most of what they needed from one quarry near the center of the island, a place now called the Blue Hole. It's one of the few spots in all the Lower Keys where a substantial amount of fresh rainwater collects, and it is a crucial source of drinking water for the island's wildlife, particularly the Key deer. Highway 940, also called Key Deer Boulevard, cuts a northern path through hardwood hammocks and pinelands, bisecting the largest of the designated Key Deer Refuge areas. The Blue Hole is just off 940 on the left, a mile and a quarter from Highway 1.

A short loop trail leads into the hammock from the back side of the Blue Hole. I am impressed at how determined the plant life is around here. Buttonwood, palmetto, slash pines (for which Big Pine Key was named), and gumbo-limbo trees grow right out of the rock with virtually no topsoil. A variety of orchids and air plants use both living and fallen trees as hosts.

This is a good place to see a Key deer, as is **No Name Key**, particularly around sunset. The first time I saw one was on No Name Key. It was a doe about the size of a springer spaniel. She sauntered across the road up ahead of me, stopped for a moment to scratch one of her oversize ears with a hind hoof, took an uninterested glance at me, then trotted off into the woods.

On your way to No Name Key (follow the signs up Wilder Road), you should stop to see one of these islands' most notable landmarks, the No Name Pub, just on the Big Pine Key side of the bridge over to No Name Key. Watch carefully for it on the left. Mangroves and cactus half conceal the clapboard building, but a hand-painted sign nailed to a palm tree tells you it's there.

Built in 1936, the No Name Pub was originally a Cuban trading post and general store. It was also reputed to have been a smuggler's hangout/hideout and a brothel. Since the mid-1970s, it's been a bar and restaurant, the oldest on the island. Inside, the No Name Pub upholds the Keys' dive bar–decor tradition of stapling signed and dated dollar bills all over the walls and ceiling. Patrons have also carved their initials in the bar, which was built using salvaged scrap from the old wooden No Name Key bridge (now replaced with a sturdier concrete crossing). This place has some of the best pizza in the Keys.

DIRECTIONS: Thirty-five miles north of Key West on Highway A1A.

DON'T MISS: Key deer (But, please, don't feed them, and do drive slowly!)
ADDRESSES AND EVENTS: See page 210–211

CONCLUSION
Bests, Mosts, and Favorites

*I*NVARIABLY, AT BOOK SIGNINGS AND AUTHOR APPEARANCES, I'm asked which town is the quaintest, which is the most scenic, or which has the best food or the best antiques shopping or the best bed-and-breakfast. At first I resisted picking favorites. After all, these would just be my personal choices, and, frankly, those change from time to time. Eventually I caved in and started answering. So here's a selection, subject to change, of course.

The prettiest, most quaint, and most romantic small town has to be Mount Dora. No doubt, the hilly terrain and numerous parks add considerably to the charm of this community.

Most artistic has to be Lake Placid, with its many building-side murals.

Choosing the best accommodations depends on what you're in the mood for. The colorful beach cottages of Seaside, the regal Herlong Mansion bed-and-breakfast in Micanopy, and Steinhatchee Landings Resort all get high marks from me.

The most interesting person I met while researching the various volumes of *Visiting Small-Town Florida* was Evinston resident Jake Glisson, artist, author, and childhood neighbor of Marjorie Rawlings.

Ma Barker thought Ocklawaha was the best hideaway, but that ultimately backfired on her. Chokoloskee or Bokeelia gets my vote.

Best place to spend Halloween: Cassadaga.

In the best architecture category, there are spectacular, century-old Victorians in DeFuniak Springs and Apalachicola, but I have to give the edge to Seaside and its colorful and imaginative Florida beach-cottage style, despite the fact that the oldest cottage there was built in 1982.

The funkiest old Florida hotel, the Island Hotel in Cedar Key, is also where you're most likely to run into someone famous trying to be incognito.

High Springs is the best home base for exploring Florida's scenic rivers.

The smallest small town is Two Egg (population: thirty-one).

The best towns for antiquing are Arcadia, High Springs, Havana, and Micanopy.

I found some terrific places to get a home-cooked meal: Flora and Ella's in La Belle, and H & F in Jasper. But Wheeler's in Arcadia tops my list. Wheeler's gets my vote for best vanilla peanut butter pie too.

The best Key lime pie is at Manny & Isa's in Islamorada.

My favorite restaurant, excluding those already mentioned, is . . . hmmm, this is tough . . . Bud & Alley's at Seaside or The Owl Café in Apalachicola.

My favorite gallery is The Crossed Palms Gallery in Bokeelia on Pine Island. Owner Nancy Brooks has an unbeatable knack for collecting wonderful art that conveys all that is beautiful about Florida.

My favorite general store? It's a toss-up among the Little River General Store in Havana, the Lawrence Grocery in Two Egg, and the Wood & Swink Store in Evinston.

My favorite beach town . . . tough choice among St. George Island, Boca Grande, and Anna Maria, but I give the edge to Anna Maria.

My favorite backroads drive is along Istachatta Road/Citrus County CR 39 from Floral City to Istachatta.

My favorite laid-back tropical getaway is Captiva.

The places you're most likely to run into a ghost are Inez's room at the Herlong Mansion in Micanopy, or anywhere in Cassadaga.

The most magical place (no, it's not Disney World) is Cross Creek. I felt Marjorie Rawlings' presence from the moment I walked through that rusty gate. It was as if she had been there just moments before I arrived. I almost expected Ida, her maid, to walk out onto the porch and tell me, "You just missed her. She walked down to the Glissons' to borrow a cup of sugar, but she'll be right back."

If you have a favorite small town in Florida that I didn't cover, or a favorite place that I didn't mention (a store, inn, or restaurant perhaps), please feel free to write to me in care of Pineapple Press, P.O. Box 3889, Sarasota, Florida 34230-3889.

Happy exploring!

APPENDIX
Addresses and Events

NORTH REGION

MILTON AND BAGDAD

Arcadia Mill Site Museum
5709 Mill Pond Road
Milton, FL 32583
(850) 626-4433

Bagdad Village Preservation
Association Museum
4512 Church Street
Bagdad, FL 32530
(850) 626-0985

Santa Rosa Chamber of Commerce
5247 Stewart Street
Milton, FL 32570
(850) 623-2339
www.srcchamber.com

Santa Rosa Historical Society
6866 Caroline Street
Milton, FL 32570
(850) 626-9830
www.santarosahistoricalsociety.org

West Florida Railroad Museum
206 Henry Street

Milton, FL 32570
(850) 623-3645

Events:
Black Water River Festival, second
weekend in March, (850) 623-2339.
Depot Days Arts & Crafts Festival,
second weekend in November, (850)
626-9830.

DEFUNIAK SPRINGS

The Big Store
782 Baldwin Avenue
DeFuniak Springs, FL 32435
(850) 892-7008

The Bookstore
640 Baldwin Avenue
DeFuniak Springs, FL 32435
(850) 892-3119

Busy Bee Café
35 South 7th Street
DeFuniak Springs, FL 32435
(850) 892-6700

Murray's Café
660 Baldwin Avenue
DeFuniak Springs, FL 32435
(850) 951-9941

Southeby's Antiques Gallery
27 Crescent Drive
DeFuniak Springs, FL 32435
(850) 892-6292

Walton County Chamber of
Commerce
Chautauqua Building
95 Circle Drive
DeFuniak Springs, FL 32435
(850) 892-3191
www.waltoncountychamber.com

Walton-DeFuniak Public Library
3 Circle Drive
DeFuniak Springs, FL 32435
(850) 892-3624

Events:
Chautauqua Festival, last Saturday in
April, (850) 892-3191.

TWO EGG

Lawrence Grocery
3972 Hwy 69A/Wintergreen Road
Two Egg, FL 32443
(850) 592-6172

Robert E. Long Cane Syrup
3911 Hwy 69
Two Egg, FL 32443
(850) 592-8012

Events:
Cane Syrup Get-together (sausage,
biscuits, and syrup; barbecue), usually the first weekend in December,
Robert E. Long Cane Syrup, (850)
592-8012

QUINCY

The Allison House Inn
215 North Madison Street
Quincy, FL 32351
(850) 875-2511
(888) 904-2511
www.allisonhouseinn.com

Gadsden County Chamber of
Commerce
P.O. Box 389
Quincy, FL 32351
(850) 627-9231
(800) 627-9231
www.gadsdencc.com

Gadsden Arts Center
Bell & Bates Hardware Store
Building
13 North Madison Street
Quincy, FL 32351
(850) 875-4866
www.gadsdenarts.com

McFarlin House Bed
& Breakfast Inn
305 East King Street
Quincy, FL 32351
(850) 875-2526
(877) 370-4701
www.mcfarlinhouse.com

The Quincy Music Theatre
Leaf Theatre Building
118 East Washington Street
Quincy, FL 32351
(850) 875-9444
www.qmtonline.com

HAVANA

Beare's Books 'N Things
101 West Seventh Avenue
Havana, FL 32333
(850) 539-5040

The Cannery
115 East Eighth Avenue
Havana, FL 32333
(850) 539-3800

H & H Antiques
302 North Main Street
Havana, FL 32333
(850) 539-6886

Little River General Store
308 North Main Street
Havana, FL 32333
(850) 539-6900
www.littlerivergs.com

McLauchlin House
201 South Seventh Avenue
Havana, FL 32333
(850) 539-3333

Mirror Image Antiques
303 First Street NW
Havana, FL 32333
(850) 539-7422

Nicholson Farmhouse Restaurant
SR 12
Havana, FL 32333
(850) 539-5931
www.nicholsonfarmhouse.com

SEASIDE

Bow Wow Meow
Central Square
Seaside, FL 32459
(850) 231-4917

Bud and Alley's Restaurant
Cinderella Circle
CR 30A
Seaside, FL 32459
(850) 231-5900
www.budandalleys.com

Café Spiazzia
Seaside, FL 32459
(850) 231-1297

Go Fish Outfitters
Central Square
Seaside, FL 32459
(850) 231-1717

Hurricane Oyster Bar
Seaside, FL 32459
(850) 534-0376

Josephine's Bed & Breakfast
38 Seaside Avenue
Seaside, FL 32459
B & B reservations: (850) 231-1940
Dining: (850) 231-1939
www.josephinesinn.com

Modica Market
Central Square
Seaside, FL 32459
(850) 231-1241
www.modicamarket.com

Pickles Beachside Grill
Seaside, FL 32459
(850) 231-5686

Roly Poly Rolled Sandwiches
Seaside, FL 32459
(850) 231-3799

Seaside Bike Shop
Central Square
Seaside, FL 32459
(850) 231-2314

Seaside Community Realty
CR 30A
Seaside, FL 32459
(850) 231-4224
www.seasidefl.com

Seaside Cottage Rental Agency
CR 30A
Seaside, FL 32459
(800) 277-8696
(850) 231-2222
www.seasidefl.com

The Seaside Institute
30 Smolian Circle, 2nd Floor
Seaside, FL 32459
(850) 231-1884
www.theseasideinstitute.org

Sundog Books
98 Central Square
Seaside, FL 32459
(850) 231-5481

Events:
Call (850) 231-5424

CARRABELLE, ST. GEORGE ISLAND,
AND APALACHICOLA

Anchor Vacation Properties
St. George Island
(800) 824-0416
www.florida-beach.com

Apalachicola Bay Chamber of
Commerce
99 Market Street
Apalachicola, FL 32320
(850) 653-9419
www.baynavigator.com

Boss Oyster Restaurant
125 Water Street
Apalachicola, FL 32320
(850) 653-9364
www.apalachicolariverinn.com/
boss.htm

Collins Vacation Rentals
St. George Island
(800) 423-7418
www.collinsvacationrentals.com

The Consulate Suites
76 Water Street
Apalachicola, FL 32320
(850) 653-1515
(877) 239-1159
www.consulatesuites.com

Coombs House Inn B & B
80 6th Street
Apalachicola, FL 32320
(850) 653-9199
www.combshouseinn.com

Gibson Inn
51 Avenue C
P.O. Box 221
Apalachicola, FL 32320-0221
(850) 653-2191
www.gibsoninn.com

The Grady Market
76 Water Street
Apalachicola, FL 32320
(850) 653-4099
www.gradymarket.com

John Gorrie State Museum
P.O. Box 267
46 6th Street
Apalachicola, FL 32320
(850) 653-9347

Julian G. Bruce/St. George Island
State Park
St. George Island, FL 32328
(850) 927-2111

Julia Mae's Seafood Restaurant
West Hwy 98
Carrabelle, FL 32322
(850) 697-3791

Owl Café
15 Avenue D
Apalachicola, FL 32320
(850) 653-9888

Prudential Resort Realty
St. George Island
(800) 332-5196
www.stgeorgeisland.com

Tamara's Floridita Café
17 Avenue E
Apalachicola, FL 32320
(850) 653-4111

Wefing's Marine and Nautical Supply
252 Water Street
Apalachicola, FL 32320
(850) 653-9218
www.wefings.com

Events:
Apalachicola Antique and Classic
Boat Show, fourth weekend in April,
(850) 653-9419

WAKULLA SPRINGS

Edward Ball Wakulla Springs State
Park and Lodge
550 Wakulla Park Drive
Wakulla Springs, FL 32327
Lodge (850) 224-5950
Park (850) 922-3632

ST. MARKS AND SOPCHOPPY

Backwoods Pizza/Sopchoppy
Outfitters
106 Municipal Avenue
Sopchoppy, FL
(850) 962-2220

Posey's Oyster Bar
P.O. Box 112
St. Marks, FL 32355
(850) 925-6172
www.poseys.com

St. Marks National Wildlife Refuge
P.O. Box 68
St. Marks, FL 32355
(850) 925-6121

Sweet Magnolia Inn Bed & Breakfast
803 Port Leon Drive
St. Marks, FL 32355
(850) 925-7670
(800) 779-5214
www.sweetmagnolia.com

Events:
Sopchoppy Worm Gruntin' Festival,
second weekend in April, (850) 962-
5282

JASPER

H & F Restaurant
Hatley Street and 2nd Avenue
Jasper, FL 32052
(386) 792-3074

WHITE SPRINGS

American Canoe Adventures
10610 Bridge Street
White Springs, FL 32096
(386) 397-1309
(800) 624-8081 (reservations only)
www.aca1.com

Nature & Heritage Tourism Center
P.O. Box 849
10903 Lillian Saunders Drive
White Springs, FL 32096
(386) 397-4461

Stephen Foster State Folk Culture
Center/State Park
P.O. Drawer G
White Springs, FL 32096
(386) 397-4331
www.stephenfostercenter.com

Events:
Annual Florida Folk Festival at the
Stephen Foster State Folk Culture
Center, fourth weekend in May,
(386) 397-2733

KEATON BEACH, DEKLE BEACH,
AND ADAMS BEACH

Keaton Beach Hot Dog Stand
21239 Keaton Beach Drive
Keaton Beach, FL 32348
(850) 578-2675
www.keatonbeach-florida.com

STEINHATCHEE

Steinhatchee Landing Resort
P.O. Box 789
Hwy 51 North
Steinhatchee, FL 32359
(352) 498-3513
www.steinhatcheelanding.com

HIGH SPRINGS

Blue Springs
CR 340
High Springs, FL 32643
(386) 454-1369

Burch Antiques
60 North Main Street
High Springs, FL 32643
(386) 454-1500

Ginnie Springs
7300 NE Ginnie Springs Road
High Springs, FL 32643
(386) 454-2202

The Grady House Bed & Breakfast
420 NW 1st Avenue
High Springs, FL 32655
(386) 454-2206
www.gradyhouse.com

Great Outdoors Trading Company
and Café
Theatre of Memory
65 Main Street
High Springs, FL 32643
(386) 454-2900
www.greatoutdoorscafe.com

Heartstrings Antiques
135 North Main Street
High Springs, FL 32655
(386) 454-4018

High Springs Chamber of Commerce
P.O. Box 863
High Springs, FL 32643
(386) 454-3120
www.highsprings.com

High Springs Antiques Center
145 North Main Street
High Springs, FL 32655
(386) 454-4770

Ichetucknee Springs State Park
Route 2, Box 108
Fort White, FL 32038
(386) 497-2511

Poe Springs Park
2880 North West 182nd Avenue
High Springs, FL 32643
(386) 454-1992

The Rustic Inn Bed & Breakfast
3105 South Main Street
High Springs, FL 32643
(386) 454-1223
www.rusticinn.net

Santa Fe River Canoe Outpost
Hwy 441 at Santa Fe River Bridge
(386) 454-2510
www.santaferiver.com

Wisteria Cottage Antiques
225 North Main Street
High Springs, FL 32655
(386) 454-8447

CROSS CREEK, EVINSTON, MICANOPY, AND MCINTOSH

Antiques Mall Downtown
110 NE Cholokka Boulevard
Micanopy, FL 32667
(352) 466-3456

Baytree Antiques
P.O. Box 490
NE Cholokka Boulevard
Micanopy, FL 32667
(352) 466-3946

First Stop Antiques
302 NE Cholokka Boulevard
Micanopy, FL 32667
(352) 466-1085

The Garage at Micanopy
212 NE Cholokka Boulevard
Micanopy, FL 32667
(352) 466-0614

Herlong Mansion
402 NE Cholokka Boulevard
Micanopy, FL 32667
(352) 466-3322
(800) 437-5664
www.herlong.com

Marjorie Kinnan Rawlings State
Historic Site
18700 South CR 325
Cross Creek/Hawthorne, FL 32640
(352) 466-3672

McIntosh Railroad Depot Historical
Museum
5500 Avenue G
McIntosh, FL 32664

The Merrily Bed & Breakfast
5802 Avenue G
McIntosh, FL 32664
(352) 591-1180

The Micanopy Country Store
202 NE Cholokka Boulevard

Micanopy, FL 32667
(352) 466-0510

Micanopy Historical Society
Museum
NE Cholokka Boulevard
Micanopy, FL 32667
(352) 488-3200
www.afn.org/~micanopy

O. Brisky Books
NE Cholokka Boulevard
P.O. Box 585
Micanopy, FL 32667
(352) 466-3910

Old Florida Café
203 NE Cholokka Boulevard
Micanopy, FL 32667
(352) 466-3663

The Twisted Sister Vintage Clothing
108 NE Cholokka Boulevard
Micanopy, FL 32667
(352) 466-4040

Wood & Swink Store and Post Office
18320 SE CR 225
Evinston, FL 32633

The Yearling Restaurant
14531 East CR 325
Cross Creek/Hawthorne, FL 32640
(352) 466-3999

Events:
McIntosh's 1890s Festival, third or
fourth weekend in October, (352)
591-1180

CRESCENT CITY AND WELAKA

Andersen's Lodge
10 Boston Street
Welaka, FL 32193
(386) 467-3344

Bass Haven Lodge & Restaurant
1 Mill Street
Welaka, FL 32193
(386) 467-8812
www.basshaven.com

Floridian Sports Club
P.O. Box 730
Welaka, FL 32193
(386) 467-2181
www.floridiansportsclub.com

Lure's Restaurant
10 Boston Street
Welaka, FL 32193
(386) 467-9310

The Shoppes at Total Interiors
334 Central Avenue
Crescent City, FL 32112
(386) 698-3420

Events:
St. Johns River Catfish Festival
(Crescent City), first weekend in
April

CEDAR KEY

Cedar Key Area Chamber of
Commerce
P.O. Box 610
Cedar Key, FL 32625

(352) 543-5600
www.cedarkey.org

Cedar Keyhole
457 2nd Street
Cedar Key, FL 32625
(352) 543-5801

Cedar Key Historical Society
Museum
P.O. Box 222
7070 D Street
Cedar Key, FL 32625
(352) 543-5549

Cedar Key State Museum
1710 Museum Drive
Cedar Key, FL 32625
(352) 543-5350

Island Hotel
373 2nd Street
Cedar Key, FL 32625
(352) 543-5111
(800) 432-4640
www.islandhotel-cedarkey.com

The Natural Experience Gallery
334 2nd Street
Cedar Key, FL 32625
(352) 543-9933

Pat's Red Luck Café
490 Dock Street
Cedar Key, FL 32625
(352) 543-6840

Pen Names Bookstore
498 2nd Street
Cedar Key, FL 32625
(352) 543-6789
www.pennamesbookstore.com

Sawgrass Gallery/Sawgrass Motel
471 Dock Street
Cedar Key, FL 32625
(352) 543-5007

The Suwannee Triangle Gallery
491 Dock Street
Cedar Key, FL 32625
(352) 543-5744
www.suwanneetriangle.com

The Water's Edge and Island
Gallery/Wild Women Gallery
470 Dock Street
Cedar Key, FL 32625
(352) 543-5710

Sidewalk Arts & Crafts Festival, second or third weekend in April, (352) 543-5600. Seafood Festival, third weekend in October, (352) 543-5600

CENTRAL REGION

YANKEETOWN

Izaak Walton Lodge and
The Compleat Angler Restaurant
1 63rd Street
Yankeetown, FL 34498
(352) 447-2311
(800) 611-5758
www.izaakwaltonlodge.com

DUNNELLON

K. P. Hole Park
SW 190th Avenue
Dunnellon, FL 34430-1772

(352) 489-3055
canoe and tube rentals

Rainbow Springs State Park
19158 SW 81st Place
Dunnellon, FL 34431
(352) 489-5803

OCKLAWAHA

Gator Joe's Beach Bar and Grill
12431 SE 135th Avenue
Oklawaha, FL 32183
(352) 288-3100

Lake Weir Chamber of Commerce
13125 SE CR 25
Oklawaha, FL 32183
(352) 288-3751

CASSADAGA AND LAKE HELEN

Cassadaga Camp Bookstore
1112 Stevens Street
Cassadaga, FL 32706
(386) 228-2880

Cassadaga Grocery Store/Café
1083 Stevens Street
Cassadaga, FL 32706
(386) 228-3797

Cassadaga Hotel
355 Cassadaga Road
Cassadaga, FL 32706
(386) 228-2323
www.cassadagahotel.com

Clauser's Inn Bed & Breakfast
201 East Kicklighter Road
Lake Helen, FL 32744
(386) 228-2337
(800) 220-0310
www.clauserinn.com

Lost in Time Café
355 Cassadaga Road
Cassadaga, FL 32706
(386) 228-2323

MOUNT DORA

Amish Cupboard and Country Stuff
122 East 4th Avenue
Mount Dora, FL 32757
(352) 385-1307

Dickens-Reed Bookshop
140 West 5th Avenue
Mount Dora, FL 32757
(352) 735-5950

Donnelly House
550 North Donnelly Street
Mount Dora, FL 32757

Eclectic Avenue
418 North Donnelly Street
Mount Dora, FL 32757
(352) 735-5069

5th Avenue Stained Glass
110 5th Avenue
Mount Dora, FL 32757
(352) 735-1934

The Gables Restaurant
322 Alexander Street

Mount Dora, FL 32757
(352) 383-8993

La Cremerie
425 North Donnelly Street
Mount Dora, FL 32757
(352) 735-4663

Lakeside Inn
100 North Alexander Street
Mount Dora, FL 32757
(352) 383-4101
(800) 556-5016
www.lakeside-inn.com

Mount Dora Area Chamber of
Commerce
Old Seaboard Coast Line Depot
341 North Alexander Street
Mount Dora, FL 32757
(352) 383-2165
www.mountdora.com

Mount Dora Lawn Bowling Club
P.O. Box 102
125 Edgerton Court
Mount Dora, FL 32756
(352) 383-4198

Odom's Interiors
352 North Alexander Street
Mount Dora, FL 32757
(352) 383-2436

Oliver Twist Antiques
404 North Donnelly Street
Mount Dora, FL 32757
(352) 735-3337

Palm Tree Grill
351 North Donnelly Street

Mount Dora, FL 32757
(352) 735-1936

Park Bench Restaurant
116 East 5th Avenue
Mount Dora, FL 32757
(352) 383-7004
www.parkbenchrestaurant.com

Piece of Mind Boutique
144 West 4th Avenue
Mount Dora, FL 32757
(352) 735-2200

Piglet's Pantry
400 North Donnelly Street
Mount Dora, FL 32757
(352) 735-9779
www.pigletspantry.com

Windsor Rose English Tea Room
144 West 4th Avenue
Mount Dora, FL 32757
(352) 735-2551

Events:
Mount Dora Art Festival, first week-
end in February. Festival of Exotic
and Antique Cars, third weekend in
February. Antique Boat Festival,
fourth weekend in March. Sailing
Regatta, April (dates vary). Bicycle
Festival, second weekend in October.
Crafts Fair, fourth weekend in
October. Christmas Celebration,
entire month of December. Call
Mount Dora Area Chamber of
Commerce for information on all
events (see above).

INVERNESS

Angelo's Pizza
West Main Street
Inverness, FL 34450
At Wick's End
101 Courthouse Square
Inverness, FL 34450
(352) 344-2583

Citrus County Chamber of
Commerce
208 West Main Street
Inverness, FL 34450
(352) 726-2801

Citrus County Historical Society
One Courthouse Square
Inverness, FL 34450
(352) 341-6427

Coach's Restaurant
West Main Street
Inverness, FL 34450

Country at Home
409 Courthouse Square
Inverness, FL 34450
(352) 637-6333
www.countryathome.foragift.com

The Crown Hotel
109 North Seminole Avenue
Inverness, FL 34450
(352) 344-5555

Old Courthouse Heritage Museum
One Courthouse Square
Inverness, FL 34450
(352) 341-6429

Rails to Trails of the Withlacoochee
Citizen's Support Organization
P.O. Box 807
Inverness, FL 34451-0807
(352) 726-2251

Ritzy Rags and Glitzy Jewels
105 Courthouse Square
Inverness, FL 34450
(352) 637-6621

Sandy Bottom Bayou
101 West Main Street
Inverness, FL 34450
(352) 341-2171

Stumpknockers Restaurant
West Main Street
Inverness, FL 34450
(352) 726-2212

Vanishing Breeds
105 West Main Street
Inverness, FL 34450
(352) 726-0024

Withlacoochee State Trail
12549 State Park Boulevard
Clermont, FL 34711
(352) 394-2280

Events:
Festival of the Arts, first or second
weekend in November, (352) 726-
2801

**FLORAL CITY, PINEOLA,
ISTACHATTA, AND NOBLETON**

Istachatta General Store
28198 Istachatta Road (Lingle Road)

Istachatta, FL 34636
(352) 544-1017

Nobleton Boat Rental Outpost
Lake Lindsey Road
Nobleton, FL 34661
(352) 796-7176
(800) 783-5284

Riverside Restaurant & Bar
29250 Lake Lindsey Road
Nobleton, FL 34661
(352) 796-9669

Events:
Strawberry Festival (Floral City), first
weekend in March, (352) 726-2801
Heritage Days, (352) 637-9925

**ARIPEKA, BAYPORT,
CHASSAHOWITZKA, AND OZELLO**

Aripeka Bait and Tackle Store
Pasco CR 595
Aripeka, FL 34679

Captain Hook's Restaurant
13982 Ozello Trail
Ozello, FL 34429
(352) 795-6900

Chassahowitzka Hotel
8551 West Miss Maggie Road
Chassahowitzka, FL 34448
(352) 382-2075
www.chazhotel.com

Chassahowitzka National
Wildlife Refuge
(352) 563-2088
www.nccentral.com/fcnwr.htm

Chassahowitzka River Campground
and Recreational Area
8600 West Miss Maggie Road
Chassahowitzka, FL 34448
(352) 382-2200

Harpozello Nature Studios
1370 Estuary Road
Ozello, FL 34429

Peck's Old Port Cove Seafood
Restaurant and Blue Crab Farm
139 North Ozello Trail
Ozello, FL 34429
(352) 795-2806

WEBSTER

E. C. Rowell Public Library/Civil
War Museum
85 East Central Avenue
Webster, FL 33597

Webster Flea Market
516 NW 3rd Street
Webster, FL 33597
(800) 832-3477
www.websterfleamarket.net

Events:
Annual Pepper Festival, third weekend in May, (352) 793-7541 or (352)
793-2073

TRILBY AND LACOOCHEE

Little Brown Church of the South
CR 575
Trilby, FL 33593

DADE CITY

Church Street Antiques
14117 8th Street
Dade City, FL 33525
(352) 523-2422

Glades Pottery and Gallery
37850 Meridian Avenue
Dade City, FL 33525
(352) 523-0992

Grapevine Antiques
37834 Meridian Avenue
Dade City, FL 33525
(352) 567-3397

Greater Dade City Chamber of
Commerce
38035 Meridian Avenue
Dade City, FL 33525
(352) 567-3769

Lunch on Limoges Restaurant
14139 7th Street
Dade City, FL 33525
(352) 567-5685

The Picket Fence
37843 Meridian Avenue
Dade City, FL 33525
(352) 523-1653

Pioneer Florida Museum
P.O. Box 335
15602 Pioneer Museum Road
Dade City, FL 33526
(352) 567-0262
www.pioneerfloridamuseum.org

Sandbar Market
37832 Meridian Avenue
Dade City, FL 33525
(352) 567-6818

Sugar Creek Antiques
37847 Meridian Avenue
Dade City, FL 33525
(352) 521-5706

Events: Kumquat Festival, last weekend in January, (352) 567-3769.
Pioneer Days Festival, Labor Day
weekend, (352) 567-0262

CHRISTMAS

Christmas Post Office
United States Postal Service
23580 East Colonial Drive (SR 50)
Christmas, FL 32709-9998
(407) 568-2941

Fort Christmas Historical Park
1300 Fort Christmas Road (SR 420)
Christmas, FL 32709
(407) 568-4149

Fort Christmas Historical Society
(407) 568-4149

Events:
Fort Christmas Bluegrass Festival and
Craft Fair, third weekend in March,
(407) 568-4149. Fort Christmas
Homecoming, first weekend in
October, (407) 568-4149. Cracker
Christmas Festival, first weekend in
December, (407) 568-4149

YEEHAW JUNCTION

Desert Inn
5570 South Kenansville Road
Intersection of Hwy 441 and SR 60
Yeehaw Junction, FL 34972
(407) 436-1054

Events:
Bluegrass Festival, second or third
weekend in January. July Fourth
BBQ. Call the Desert Inn for exact
dates

ANNA MARIA AND HOLMES BEACH

Anna Maria Island Chamber of
Commerce
501 Manatee Avenue, Suite D
Holmes Beach, FL 34217-1991
(941) 778-1541

Anna Maria Island Historical Society
Anna Maria Island Museum
P.O. Box 4315
402 Pine Avenue
Anna Maria, FL 34216
(941) 778-0492

Beach Bistro Restaurant
6600 Gulf Drive
Holmes Beach, FL 34217
(941) 778-6444
www.beachbistro.com

City Pier Restaurant at the Anna
Maria City Pier
100 South Bay Boulevard
Anna Maria, FL 34216
(941) 779-1667

Duffy's Tavern
5808 Marina Drive
Holmes Beach, Florida 34217
(941) 778-2501

Harrington House Beachfront Bed &
Breakfast
5626 Gulf Drive
Holmes Beach, FL 34217
(941) 778-5444
(888) 828-5566
www.harringtonhouse.com

Mr. Bones BBQ
3007 Gulf Drive
Holmes Beach, FL 34217
(941) 778-6614

Ooh La La European Bistro
Island Shopping Center
5406 Marina Drive
Holmes Beach, FL 34217
(941) 778-5320

Rod and Reel Pier Café
875 North Shore Drive
Anna Maria, FL 34216
(941) 778-1885

Sandbar Restaurant
100 Spring Avenue
Anna Maria, FL 34216
(941) 778-0444

Sign of the Mermaid Restaurant
9707 Gulf Drive
Anna Maria, FL 34216
(941) 778-9399

CORTEZ

Annie's Bait and Tackle
4334 127th Street West
Cortez, FL 34215
(941) 794-3580

Manatee Chamber of Commerce
P.O. Box 321
222 10th Street West
Bradenton, FL 34206
(941) 748-3411

N. E. Taylor Boatworks
c/o Alcee Taylor
P.O. Box 41
Cortez, FL 34215

Sea Hagg Nauticals
12304 Cortez Road
Cortez, FL 34215
(941) 795-5756
www.seahagg.com

Events:
Cortez Fishing Festival, third weekend in February, (941) 795-4637

LAKE PLACID

Archbold Biological Station
P.O. Box 2057
Old SR 8
Lake Placid, FL 33862
(863) 465-2571
www.archbold-station.org
   The Archbold Biological Station is
a scientific research facility dedicated
to studying the behavior, ecology, and
conservation of native south Florida

animals and plants. Group tours can be arranged by appointment.

Caladium Arts and Crafts Co-op
24 Interlake Boulevard
Lake Placid, FL 33852
(863) 699-5940

Clown College Museum
112 West Interlake Boulevard
Lake Placid, FL 33852
www.tobytheclownfoundationinc.com

Fancy Leaf Caladiums
Happiness Farms
704 CR 621 East
Lake Placid, FL 33852
(863) 465-0044

Greater Lake Placid Chamber of
Commerce
18 North Oak Street
Lake Placid, FL 33852
(863) 465-4331
www.lpfla.com

Lake Placid Historical Society
Museum
19 West Park Avenue
Lake Placid, FL 33852
(863) 465-1771
    The Historical Society Museum is in the refurbished Atlantic Coast Railroad depot.

Lake Placid Mural Society
18 North Oak Street
Lake Placid, FL 33852
(863) 465-2394

Main Street America Restaurant
22 South Main Street
Lake Placid, FL 33852
(863) 465-7733

Placid Tower
Tower Plaza
Hwy 27
Lake Placid, FL 33852
(863) 465-3310

Events:
Lake Placid Arts and Crafts County Fair, February. Caladium Festival, August. Call Greater Lake Placid Chamber of Commerce for exact dates.

ARCADIA

Arcadia Rodeo Association
124 Heard Street
Arcadia, FL 34266
(800) 749-7633

Arcadia Tea Room
117 West oak Street
Arcadia, FL 34266
(863) 494-2424

Brenda Lee's Deli Café
26 West Oak Street
Arcadia, FL 34266
(863) 494-3898

DeSoto County Chamber of
Commerce
16 South Volusia Avenue
Arcadia, FL 34266
(863) 494-4033

Heard Opera House Museum
106 West Oak Street
Arcadia, FL 34266
(863) 494-7010

Historic Parker House Bed &
Breakfast
427 West Hickory Street
Arcadia, FL 34266
(863) 494-2499
(800) 969-2499
www.historicparkerhouse.com

Hot Fudge Shoppe
10 South Polk Street
Arcadia, FL 34266
(863) 494-6633

Wheeler's Goody Café
13 South Monroe Avenue
Arcadia, FL 34266
(863) 993-1555

Events:
Arcadia Rodeo, second weekend in
March. Call Arcadia Rodeo
Association for information.

SOUTH REGION

BOCA GRANDE

Boca Grande Area Chamber of
Commerce
P.O. Box 704
Boca Grande, FL 33921
(941) 964-0568
www.bocagrandechamber.com

Boca Grande Baking
Company/Coffee Shop
384 East Railroad Avenue
Boca Grande, FL 33921
(941) 964-5818

Boca Grande Fishing Guides
Association
P.O. Box 676
Boca Grande, FL 33921
(800) 667-1612
www.bocagrandefishing.com

Fugate's
428 West 4th Street
Boca Grande, FL 33921
(941) 964-2323

Gasparilla Inn & Cottages
P.O. Box 1088
Park Avenue and Fifth Street
Boca Grande, FL 33921
(941) 964-2201

Gasparilla Island State Recreation
Area
Historic Boca Grande Lighthouse
P.O. Box 1150
Boca Grande, FL 33921

Island Bike 'N Beach
333 Park Avenue
Boca Grande, FL 33921
(941) 964-0711
(golf cart and bike rentals)

Loon's on a Limb Restaurant
310 East Railroad Avenue
Boca Grande, FL 33921
(941) 964-0155

PJ's Seagrille
321 Park Avenue
Boca Grande, FL 33921
(941) 964-0806

The Temptation Restaurant
350 Park Avenue
Boca Grande, FL 33921
(941) 964-2610
(941) 964-2327 (bar)

Events:
World's Richest Tarpon Tournament,
second weekend in July. Call Boca
Grande Area Chamber of Commerce
for information.

LA BELLE AND CLEWISTON

Clewiston Chamber of Commerce
P.O. Box 275
544 West Sugarland Hwy (Hwy 27)
Clewiston, FL 33440
(863) 983-7979

Clewiston Inn
Everglades Lounge
108 Royal Palm Avenue
Clewiston, FL 33440
(863) 983-8151
(800) 749-4466

Flora & Ella's Restaurant
550 Hwy 80 West
La Belle, FL 33935
(863) 675-2891

Roland Martin's Marina and Resort
920 East Del Monte Avenue
Clewiston, FL 33440
(863) 983-3151

MATLACHA, BOKEELIA, ST. JAMES CITY, AND PINELAND

Cabbage Key Inn and Restaurant
P.O. Box 200
Pineland, FL 33945
(941) 283-2278

Capt'n Con's Fish House
Main Street
Bokeelia, FL 33922
(239) 283-4300

Crossed Palms Gallery
8315 Main Street
Bokeelia, FL 33922
(239) 283-2283

Greater Pine Island Chamber of
Commerce
P.O. Box 525
Matlacha, FL 33909
(239) 283-0888

Matlacha Island Cottages
4756 Pine Island Road
Matlacha, FL
Mailing address:
P.O. Box 559
Bokeelia, FL 33922
(800) 877-7256
(239) 283-7368
www.islandcottages.com

Museum of the Islands
5728 Sesame Drive
Bokeelia, FL 33922
(941) 283-1525

Randall Research Center
P.O. Box 608
Pineland, FL 33945-0608
(941) 283-2062

Tarpon Lodge
13771 Waterfront Drive
Pineland, FL 33945
(941) 283-3999
www.tarponlodge.com

The Waterfront Restaurant and
Marina
2131 Oleander Street
St. James City, FL 33956
(239) 283-0592
www.waterfrontrestaurant.com

SANIBEL AND CAPTIVA

The Bean
2240 Periwinkle Way
Sanibel Island, FL 33957
(239) 395-1919

Captiva Chapel by the Sea
11580 Chapin Street
Captiva Island, FL 33924
(239) 472-1646

The Castaways
6460 Sanibel-Captiva Road
Sanibel Island, FL 33957
(800) 375-0152
(239) 472-1252
www.castawayssanibel.com

Cheeburger Cheeburger
2413 Periwinkle Way
Sanibel Island, FL 33957
(239) 472-6111

Confused Chameleon
11528 Andy Rosse Lane
Captiva Island, FL 33924
(239) 472-0560

J. N. "Ding" Darling National Wildlife
Refuge
1 Wildlife Drive
Sanibel Island, FL 33957
(239) 472-1100

Jungle Drums Gallery
11532 Andy Rosse Lane
Captiva Island, FL 33924
(239) 395-2266
www.jungledrumsgallery.com

Mad Hatter Restaurant
6467 Sanibel-Captiva Road
Sanibel Island, FL 33957
(239) 472-0033

The Mucky Duck
11546 Andy Rosse Lane
Captiva Island, FL 33924
(239) 472-3434
www.muckyduck.com

Sanibel and Captiva Islands Chamber
of Commerce
1159 Causeway Road
Sanibel Island, FL 33957
(239) 472-1080
www.sanibel-captiva.org

Sunshine Café
14900 Captiva Drive
Captiva Island, FL 33924
(239) 472-6200

The 'Tween Waters Inn
P.O. Box 249

Captiva Island, FL 33924
(800) 223-5865
(239) 472-5161
www.tween-waters.com

ESTERO

Estero River Outfitters
20991 Hwy 41
Estero, FL 33928
(941) 992-4050
www.all-florida.com/swestero.htm

Koreshan State Historic Site
P.O. Box 7
CR 850/Corkscrew Road and
Hwy 41
Estero, FL 33928
(941) 992-0311

Koreshan Unity Foundation
P.O. Box 97
8661 Corkscrew Road (CR 850)
Estero, FL 33928
(941) 992-2184

EVERGLADES CITY, CHOKOLOSKEE,
OCHOPEE

Captain Doug House's Florida Boat
Tours
Route 29
Everglades City, FL 33929
(800) 282-9194

Clyde Butcher Big Cypress Gallery
52388 Hwy 41/Tamiami Trail
Ochopee, FL 34141
(239) 695-2428

www.clydebutcher.com

Everglades Area Chamber of
Commerce
P.O. Box 130
Everglades City, FL 34139
(800) 914-6355
(239) 695-3941

Everglades National Park
40001 SR 9336
Homestead, FL 33134-6733
or
P.O. Box 279
Homestead, FL 33030
(305) 242-7700

Everglades National Park Boat Tours
Western Water Gateway
P.O. Box 119
Everglades City, FL 34139
(239) 695-2591
(800) 445-7724

Historic Ted Smallwood's Store
P.O. Box 367
360 Mamie Street
Chokoloskee, FL 34138
(239) 695-2989

Museum of the Everglades
105 West Broadway
Everglades City, FL 34139
(239) 695-0008

Oar House Restaurant
305 North Collier Avenue
Everglades City, FL 33929
(239) 695-3535

Ochopee Post Office
Hwy 41
Ochopee, FL 34141

Rod and Gun Club
P.O. Box 190
Everglades City, FL 34139
(239) 695-2101

Events:
Everglades City Seafood Festival, first
full weekend in February.

TAVERNIER AND ISLAMORADA

Cheeca Lodge
Mile Marker 82
P.O. Box 527
Islamorada, FL 33036
(305) 664-4651
(800) 327-2888
www.cheeca.com

Green Turtle Inn
Mile Marker 81.5
Islamorada, FL 33036
(305) 664-9031
www.greenturtleinn.com

Helen Wadley Branch Library
Mile Marker 82
Islamorada, FL 33036

Historic Tavernier Hotel
Copper Kettle Restaurant
Mile marker 91.8
91865 Overseas Hwy (US Hwy 1)
Tavernier, FL 33070
(305) 852-4131

(800) 515-4131
www.tavernierhotel.com

Islamorada Chamber of Commerce
P.O. Box 915
Islamorada, FL 33036
(305) 664-4503
www.islamoradachamber.com

Manny & Isa's Kitchen
Mile Marker 81.6
81671 Overseas Hwy (US Hwy 1)
Islamorada, FL 33036
(305) 664-5019

Events:
Fishing tournaments almost every
weekend of the year. Call Islamorada
Chamber of Commerce for information.

BIG PINE KEY AND NO NAME KEY

The Barnacle Bed & Breakfast
1557 Long Beach Road
Big Pine Key, FL 33043
(305) 872-3298
(800) 465-9100
www.thebarnacle.net

Bahia Honda State Park
36850 Overseas Hwy
Big Pine Key, FL 33043
(305) 872-3210
www.bahiahondapark.com

Lower Keys Chamber of Commerce
Mile Marker 31
P.O. Box 430511
Big Pine Key, FL 33043-0511

(305) 872-2411
(800) 872-3722
www.lowerkeyschamber.com

National Key Deer Refuge/Florida
Keys National Wildlife Refuge
28950 Watson Boulevard
Big Pine Key, FL 33043
(305) 872-2239
http://nationalkeydeer.fws.gov

No Name Pub
North Watson Boulevard
Big Pine Key, FL 33043
(305) 872-9115
www.nonamepub.com

Events:
Underwater Music Festival (on the
reefs at Looe Key), second weekend
in July, (305) 872-2411

INDEX

Note: **CP** refers to color plates between pages 82 and 83.

213

NOTES

NOTES

NOTES

If you enjoyed reading this book, here are some other books from Pineapple Press on related topics. For a complete catalog, write to Pineapple Press, P.O. Box 3889, Sarasota, FL 34230 or call 1-800-PINEAPL (746-3275). Or visit our website at www.pineapplepress.com.

Best Backroads of Florida by Douglas Waitley. Each volume in this series offers several well-planned day trips through some of Florida's least-known towns and little-traveled byways. You will glimpse a gentler Florida and learn lots about its history. Volume 1: The Heartland (south of Jacksonville to north of Tampa) ISBN 1-56164-189-8 (pb). Volume 2: Coasts, Glades, and Groves (South Florida) ISBN 1-56164-232-0 (pb). Volume 3: Beaches and Hills (North and Northwest Florida).

Book Lover's Guide to Florida edited by Kevin M. McCarthy. Exhaustive survey of writers, books, and literary sites. A reference, guide for reading, and literary tour guide. ISBN 1-56164-012-3 (hb); ISBN 1-56164-021-2 (pb)

Exploring South Carolina's Islands by Terrance Zepke. A complete guide for vacationers, day-trippers, armchair travelers, and people looking to relocate to this charming area. What to see and do, where to stay and eat on South Carolina's fabled islands, with over 70 photos. ISBN 1-56164-259-2 (pb)

Florida Lighthouse Trail, ed. Thomas Taylor. A fascinating collection of the histories of Florida's light stations by different authors, each an authority on a particular lighthouse. Chock-full of information on dates of construction and operation, with complete directions to and contact information for each lighthouse. ISBN 1-56164-203-7 (pb)

Florida's Finest Inns and Bed & Breakfasts by Bruce Hunt. From warm and cozy country bed & breakfasts to elegant and historic hotels, author Bruce Hunt has composed the definitive guide to Florida's most quaint, romantic, and often eclectic lodgings. With photos and charming pen-and-ink drawings by the author. ISBN 1-56164-202-9 (pb)

Haunted Lighthouses and How to Find Them by George Steitz. The producer of the popular TV series *Haunted Lighthouses* takes you on a tour of America's most enchanting and mysterious lighthouses. ISBN 1-56164-268-1 (pb)

Hemingway's Key West Second Edition by Stuart McIver. A rousing, true-to-life portrait of Hemingway in Key West, Cuba, and Bimini during his heyday. Includes a two-hour walking tour of the author's favorite Key West haunts and a narrative of the places he frequented in Cuba. ISBN 1-56164-241-X (pb)

Historic Homes of Florida by Laura Stewart and Susanne Hupp. Seventy-four notable dwellings throughout the state—all open to the public—tell the human side of history. Each home is illustrated by H. Patrick Reed or Nan E. Wilson. ISBN 1-56164-085-9 (pb)

Houses of Key West by Alex Caemmerer. Eyebrow houses, shotgun houses, Conch Victorians, and many more styles illustrated with lavish color photographs and complemented by anecdotes about old Key West. ISBN 1-56164-009-3 (pb)

Houses of St. Augustine by David Nolan. A history of the city told through its buildings, from the earliest coquina structures, through the Colonial and Victorian times, to the modern era. Color photographs and original watercolors. ISBN 1-56164-0697 (hb); ISBN 1-56164-075-1 (pb)

Tales from a Florida Fish Camp by Jack Montrose. The author, a fish camp regular since 1965, reminisces about the good old days fishing on the St. Johns River. ISBN 1-56164-276-2 (pb)